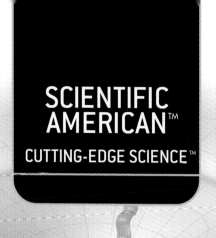

SCIENTIFIC
AMERICAN™
CUTTING-EDGE SCIENCE™

# Beyond
# Extreme Physics

ROSEN
PUBLISHING®

New York

Published in 2008 by The Rosen Publishing Group, Inc.
29 East 21st Street, New York, NY 10010

The articles in this book first appeared in the pages of *Scientific American*, as follows: "The First Few Microseconds" by Michael Riordan and William A. Zajc, May 2006; "An Echo of Black Holes" by Theodore A. Jacobson and Renaud Parentani, December 2005; "The Illusion of Gravity" by Juan Maldacena, November 2005; "The Mysteries of Mass" by Gordon Kane, July 2005; "Inconstant Constants" by John D. Barrow and John K. Webb, June 2005; "Quantum Black Holes" by Bernard J. Carr and Steven B. Giddings, May 2005; "The String Theory Landscape" by Raphael Bousso and Joseph Polchinski, September 2004.

First Edition

**Library of Congress Cataloging-in-Publication Data**

Beyond extreme physics.—1st ed.
    p. cm.—(Scientific American cutting-edge science)
Includes index.
ISBN-13: 978-1-4042-1402-6 (library binding)
1. Relativity (Physics) 2. Particles (Nuclear physics) 3. Quantum theory.
4. Gravity. 5. String models. I. Scientific American.
QC173.55.B497 2008
539—dc22
                                                    2007029541
*Manufactured in Singapore*

**On the cover:** In this picture, the size of an elephant is compared to the size of an ant, which is meant to represent the size comparison between the top quark and the neutrino.
**Background:** Scientists are studying models of black holes using sound waves. This is an artist's depiction of a black hole in a fluid-like space.

**Illustration credits:** Cover: Bryan Christie Design (foreground), Ken Brown (background); pp. 6, 7, 12, 14, 15, 18 Lucy Reading-Ikkanda; pp. 32, 40, 42, 43, 44 George Retseck; pp. 49, 68, 72, 73, 75, 78, 79 Bryan Christie Design; p. 63 Alfred T. Kamajian; pp. 94, 95, 98, 99, 104 Alison Kendall; p. 103 Alison Kendall; Source: John K. Webb; p. 109 Richard Sword; pp. 114, 119, 122, 123, 129 Don Dixon; p. 126 Don Dixon; Jana Brenning (graph); pp. 134, 138, 139, 144, 151 Don Foley.

# Table of Contents

# Introduction

Imagine a world in which spacetime is a fluid, the constants of nature change with time, and our universe is but one of a virtually infinite number of universes. Bizarre? Yes. Impossible? Not at all. Indeed, such scenarios reflect the current thinking of some of today's foremost physicists. And they are just some of the cutting-edge ideas that leading authorities explore in this book on extreme physics.

In the pages that follow, you'll also learn how researchers are re-creating the conditions of the nascent universe; why gravity and mass are still surprising; and how physicists could soon use quantum black holes to probe the extra dimensions of space. So buckle up— you're in for a mind-bending ride. —*The Editors*

# I. "The First Few Microseconds"

By Michael Riordan and William A. Zajc

*In recent experiments, physicists have replicated conditions of the infant universe—with startling results.*

For the past five years, hundreds of scientists have been using a powerful new atom smasher at Brookhaven National Laboratory on Long Island to mimic conditions that existed at the birth of the universe. Called the Relativistic Heavy Ion Collider (RHIC, pronounced "rick"), it clashes two opposing beams of gold nuclei traveling at nearly the speed of light. The resulting collisions between pairs of these atomic nuclei generate exceedingly hot, dense bursts of matter and energy to simulate what happened during the first few microseconds of the big bang. These brief "mini bangs" give physicists a ringside seat on some of the earliest moments of creation.

During those early moments, matter was an ultrahot, superdense brew of particles called quarks and gluons rushing hither and thither and crashing willy-nilly into one another. A sprinkling of electrons, photons and other light elementary particles seasoned the soup. This mixture had a temperature in the trillions of degrees, more than 100,000 times hotter than the sun's core.

But the temperature plummeted as the cosmos expanded, just like an ordinary gas cools today when

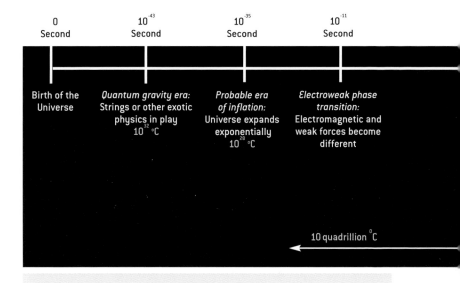

| 0 Second | $10^{-43}$ Second | $10^{-35}$ Second | $10^{-11}$ Second |
|---|---|---|---|
| Birth of the Universe | Quantum gravity era: Strings or other exotic physics in play $10^{32}$ °C | Probable era of inflation: Universe expands exponentially $10^{28}$ °C | Electroweak phase transition: Electromagnetic and weak forces become different |

10 quadrillion $^0$C

←

Cosmic timeline shows some significant eras in the early history of the universe. Experiments—SPS, RHIC and the future LHC—probe progressively further back into the first microseconds when the quark-gluon medium existed.

it expands rapidly. The quarks and gluons slowed down so much that some of them could begin sticking together briefly. After nearly 10 microseconds had elapsed, the quarks and gluons became shackled together by strong forces between them, locked up permanently within protons, neutrons and other strongly interacting particles that physicists collectively call "hadrons." Such an abrupt change in the properties of a material is called a phase transition (like liquid water freezing into ice). The cosmic phase transition from the original mix of quarks and gluons into mundane protons and neutrons is of intense interest to scientists, both those who seek clues about how the universe evolved toward its current highly

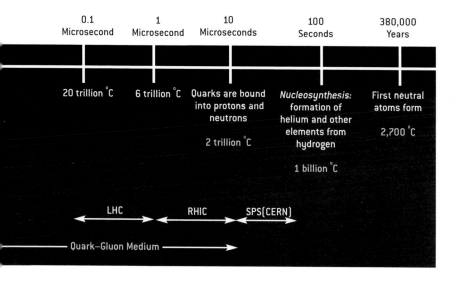

| 0.1 Microsecond | 1 Microsecond | 10 Microseconds | 100 Seconds | 380,000 Years |
|---|---|---|---|---|

20 trillion °C    6 trillion °C    Quarks are bound into protons and neutrons    *Nucleosynthesis:* formation of helium and other elements from hydrogen    First neutral atoms form

2 trillion °C    1 billion °C    2,700 °C

LHC    RHIC    SPS(CERN)

Quark–Gluon Medium

structured state and those who wish to understand better the fundamental forces involved.

The protons and neutrons that form the nuclei of every atom today are relic droplets of that primordial sea, tiny subatomic prison cells in which quarks thrash back and forth, chained forever. Even in violent collisions, when the quarks seem on the verge of breaking out, new "walls" form to keep them confined. Although many physicists have tried, no one has ever witnessed a solitary quark drifting all alone through a particle detector.

RHIC offers researchers a golden opportunity to observe quarks and gluons unchained from protons and neutrons in a collective, quasi-free state reminiscent of these earliest microseconds of existence. Theorists originally dubbed this concoction the quark-gluon plasma, because they expected it to act like an ultrahot gas of charged particles (a plasma) similar to the innards of a lightning bolt. By smashing heavy nuclei together in mini bangs that briefly liberate quarks and gluons, RHIC serves as a kind of time telescope providing glimpses of the early universe, when the ultrahot, super-dense quark-gluon plasma reigned supreme. And the greatest surprise at RHIC so far is that this exotic substance seems to be acting much more like a liquid— albeit one with very special properties—than a gas.

## Free the Quarks

In 1977, when theorist Steven Weinberg published his classic book *The First Three Minutes* about the physics of the early universe, he avoided any definitive conclusions about the first hundredth of a second. "We simply do not yet know enough about the physics of elementary particles to be able to calculate the properties of such a mélange with any confidence," he lamented. "Thus our ignorance of microscopic physics stands as a veil, obscuring our view of the very beginning."

But theoretical and experimental breakthroughs of that decade soon began to lift the veil. Not only were protons, neutrons and all other hadrons found to contain quarks; in addition, a theory of the strong force between quarks—known as quantum chromo-dynamics, or QCD—emerged in the mid-1970s. This theory postulated that a shadowy cabal of eight neutral particles called gluons flits among the quarks, carrying the unrelenting force that confines them within hadrons.

## Overview/Mini Bangs

- In the first 10 microseconds of the big bang, the universe consisted of a seething maelstrom of elementary particles known as quarks and gluons. Ever since that epoch, quarks and gluons have been locked up inside the protons and neutrons that make up the nuclei of atoms.
- For the past five years, experiments at the Relativistic Heavy Ion Collider (RHIC) have been re-creating the so-called quark-gluon plasma on a microscopic scale by smashing gold nuclei together at nearly the speed of light. To physicists' great surprise, the medium produced in these mini bangs behaves not like a gas but like a nearly perfect liquid.
- The results mean that models of the very early universe may have to be revised. Some assumptions that physicists make to simplify their computations relating to quarks and gluons also need to be reexamined.

What is especially intriguing about QCD is that—contrary to what happens with such familiar forces as gravity and electromagnetism—the coupling strength grows *weaker* as quarks approach one another. Physicists have called this curious counterintuitive behavior asymptotic freedom. It means that when two quarks are substantially closer than a proton diameter (about $10^{-13}$ centimeter), they feel a reduced force, which physicists can calculate with great precision by means of standard techniques. Only when a quark begins to stray from its partner does the force become truly strong, yanking the particle back like a dog on a leash.

In quantum physics, short distances between particles are associated with high-energy collisions. Thus, asymptotic freedom becomes important at high temperatures when particles are closely packed and constantly undergo high-energy collisions with one another.

More than any other single factor, the asymptotic freedom of QCD is what allows physicists to lift Weinberg's veil and evaluate what happened during those first few microseconds. As long as the temperature exceeded about 10 trillion degrees Celsius, the quarks and gluons acted essentially independently. Even at lower temperatures, down to two trillion degrees, the quarks would have roamed individually—although by then they would have begun to feel the confining QCD force tugging at their heels.

To simulate such extreme conditions here on earth, physicists must re-create the enormous temperatures, pressures and densities of those first few microseconds. Temperature is essentially the average kinetic energy of a particle in a swarm of similar particles, whereas pressure increases with the swarm's energy density. Hence, by squeezing the highest possible energies into the smallest possible volume we have the best chance of simulating conditions that occurred in the big bang.

Fortunately, nature provides ready-made, extremely dense nuggets of matter in the form of atomic nuclei. If you could somehow gather together a thimbleful of this nuclear matter, it would weigh 300 million tons. Three decades of experience colliding heavy nuclei such as lead and gold at high energies have shown that the densities occurring during these collisions far surpass that of normal nuclear matter. And the temperatures produced may have exceeded five trillion degrees.

Colliding heavy nuclei that each contain a total of about 200 protons and neutrons produces a much larger inferno than occurs in collisions of individual protons (as commonly used in other high-energy physics experiments). Instead of a tiny explosion with dozens of particles flying out, such heavy-ion collisions create a seething fireball consisting of thousands of particles. Enough particles are involved for the collective properties of the fireball—its temperature, density, pressure and viscosity (its thickness or resistance to flowing)—to become useful, significant parameters. The distinction is important—like the difference between the behavior of a few isolated water molecules and that of an entire droplet.

## The RHIC Experiments

Funded by the U.S. Department of Energy and operated by Brookhaven, RHIC is the latest facility for generating and studying heavy-ion collisions. Earlier nuclear accelerators fired beams of heavy nuclei at stationary metal targets. RHIC, in contrast, is a particle collider that crashes together two beams of heavy nuclei. The resulting head-on collisions generate far greater energies for the same velocity of particle because all the available energy goes into creating mayhem. This is much like what happens when two speeding cars smash head-on. Their energy of motion is converted into the random, thermal energy of parts and debris flying in almost every direction.

At the highly relativistic energies generated at RHIC, nuclei travel at more than 99.99 percent of the speed of light, reaching energies as high as 100 giga-electron volts (GeV) for every proton or neutron inside. (One GeV is about equivalent to the mass of a stationary proton.) Two strings of 870 superconducting magnets cooled by tons of liquid helium steer the beams around two interlaced 3.8-kilometer rings. The beams clash at four points where these rings cross. Four sophisticated particle detectors known as BRAHMS, PHENIX,

## Colliding and Detecting Particles

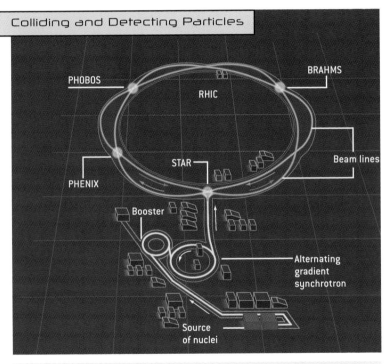

RHIC consists primarily of two 3.8-kilometer rings, or beam lines, that accelerate gold and other heavy nuclei to 0.9999 of the speed of light. The beam lines cross at six locations. At four of these intersections, the nuclei collide head-on, producing mini bangs that emulate conditions during the big bang that created the universe. Detectors known as BRAHMS, PHENIX, PHOBOS and STAR analyze the debris flying out from the collisions.

PHOBOS and STAR record the subatomic debris spewing out from the violent smashups at these collision points.

When two gold nuclei collide head-on at RHIC's highest attainable energy, they dump a total of more than 20,000 GeV into a microscopic fireball just a trillionth of a centimeter across. The nuclei and their constituent protons and neutrons literally melt, and many more quarks, antiquarks (antimatter opposites of the quarks) and gluons are created from all the energy available. More than 5,000 elementary particles are briefly liberated in typical encounters. The pressure generated at the moment of collision is truly immense, a whopping $10^{30}$ times atmospheric pressure, and the temperature inside the fireball soars into the trillions of degrees.

But about 50 trillionths of a trillionth ($5 \times 10^{-23}$) of a second later, all the quarks, antiquarks and gluons recombine into hadrons that explode outward into the surrounding detectors. Aided by powerful computers, these experiments attempt to record as much information as possible about the thousands of particles reaching them. Two of these experiments, BRAHMS and PHOBOS, are relatively small and concentrate on observing specific characteristics of the debris. The other two, PHENIX and STAR, are built around huge, general-purpose devices that fill their three-story experimental halls with thousands of tons of magnets, detectors, absorbers and shielding [see "Colliding and Detecting Particles" box].

## A Mini Bang from Start to Finish

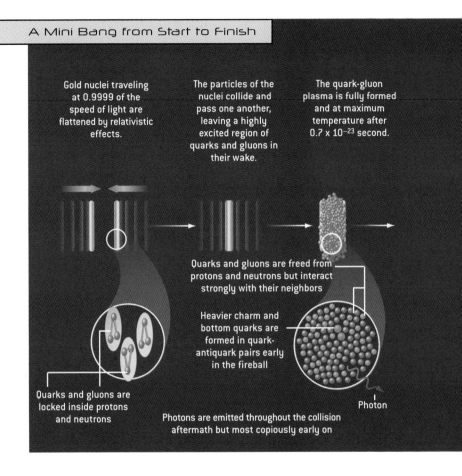

Gold nuclei traveling at 0.9999 of the speed of light are flattened by relativistic effects.

The particles of the nuclei collide and pass one another, leaving a highly excited region of quarks and gluons in their wake.

The quark-gluon plasma is fully formed and at maximum temperature after $0.7 \times 10^{-23}$ second.

Quarks and gluons are freed from protons and neutrons but interact strongly with their neighbors

Heavier charm and bottom quarks are formed in quark-antiquark pairs early in the fireball

Quarks and gluons are locked inside protons and neutrons

Photon

Photons are emitted throughout the collision aftermath but most copiously early on

RHIC generates conditions similar to the first few microseconds of the big bang by slamming together gold nuclei at nearly the speed of light. Each collision, or mini bang, goes through a series of stages, briefly producing an expanding fireball of gluons, quarks and antiquarks. The quarks and antiquarks are mostly of the up, down and strange species, with only a few of the heavier charm and bottom species. The fireball ultimately blows apart in the form of hadrons, which are detected along with photons and other decay products. Scientists deduce the physical properties of the quark-gluon medium from the properties of these detected particles.

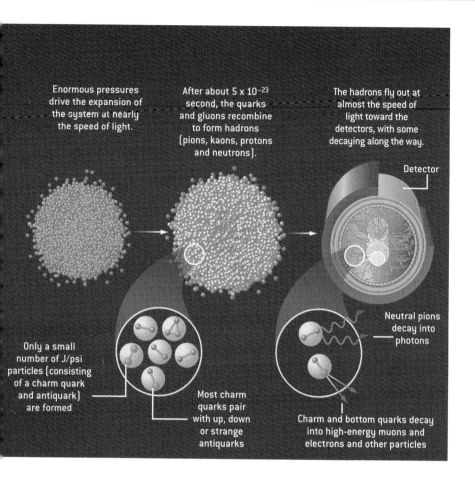

Enormous pressures drive the expansion of the system at nearly the speed of light.

After about 5 x 10⁻²³ second, the quarks and gluons recombine to form hadrons (pions, kaons, protons and neutrons).

The hadrons fly out at almost the speed of light toward the detectors, with some decaying along the way.

Detector

Neutral pions decay into photons

Only a small number of J/psi particles (consisting of a charm quark and antiquark) are formed

Most charm quarks pair with up, down or strange antiquarks

Charm and bottom quarks decay into high-energy muons and electrons and other particles

The four RHIC experiments have been designed, constructed and operated by separate international teams ranging from 60 to more than 500 scientists. Each group has employed a different strategy to address the daunting challenge presented by the enormous complexity of RHIC events. The BRAHMS collaboration elected to focus on remnants of the original protons and neutrons that speed along close to the direction of the colliding gold nuclei. In contrast, PHOBOS observes particles over the widest possible angular range and studies correlations among them. STAR was built around the world's largest "digital camera," a huge cylinder of gas that provides three-dimensional pictures of all the charged particles emitted in a large aperture surrounding the beam axis. And PHENIX searches for specific particles produced very early in the collisions that can emerge unscathed from the boiling cauldron of quarks and gluons. It thus provides a kind of x-ray portrait of the inner depths of the fireball.

## A Perfect Surprise

The physical picture emerging from the four experiments is consistent and surprising. The quarks and gluons indeed break out of confinement and behave collectively, if only fleetingly. But this hot mélange acts like a liquid, not the ideal gas theorists had anticipated.

The energy densities achieved in head-on collisions between two gold nuclei are stupendous, about 100 times those of the nuclei themselves—largely because of relativity. As viewed from the laboratory, both nuclei are relativistically flattened into ultrathin disks of protons and neutrons just before they meet. So all their energy is crammed into a very tiny volume at the moment of impact. Physicists estimate that the resulting energy density is at least 15 times what is needed to set the quarks and gluons free. These particles immediately begin darting in every direction, bashing into one another repeatedly and thereby reshuffling their energies into a more thermal distribution.

Evidence for the rapid formation of such a hot, dense medium comes from a phenomenon called jet quenching. When two protons collide at high energy, some of their quarks and gluons can meet nearly head-on and rebound, resulting in narrow, back-to-back sprays of hadrons (called jets) blasting out in opposite directions [see "Evidence for a Dense Liquid" box]. But the PHENIX and STAR detectors witness only one half of such a pair in collisions between gold nuclei. The lone jets indicate that individual quarks and gluons are indeed colliding at high energy. But where is the other jet? The rebounding quark or gluon must have plowed into the hot, dense medium just formed; its high energy would then have been dissipated by many close encounters with low-energy quarks and gluons. It is like firing a bullet into a body of water; almost all the bullet's energy is absorbed by slow-moving water molecules, and it cannot punch through to the other side.

Indications of liquidlike behavior of the quark-gluon medium came early in the RHIC experiments, in the form of a phenomenon called elliptic flow. In collisions that occur slightly off-center—which is often the case—the hadrons that emerge reach the detector in an elliptical distribution. More energetic hadrons squirt out within the plane of the interaction than at right angles to it. The elliptical pattern indicates that substantial pressure gradients must be at work in the quark-gluon medium and that the quarks and gluons from which

## Evidence for a Dense Liquid

Two phenomena in particular point to the quark-gluon medium being a dense liquid state of matter: jet quenching and elliptic flow. Jet quenching implies the quarks and gluons are closely packed, and elliptic flow would not occur if the medium were a gas.

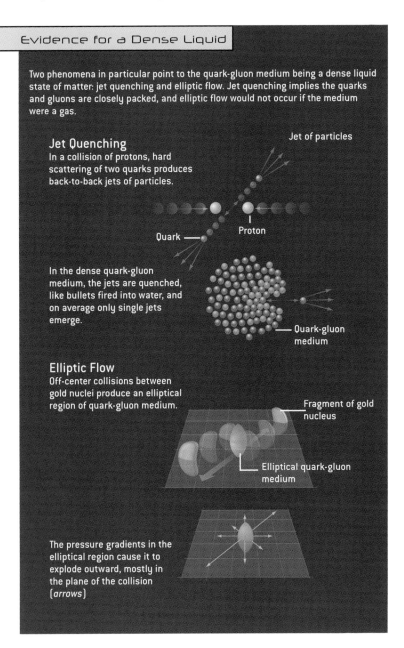

### Jet Quenching
In a collision of protons, hard scattering of two quarks produces back-to-back jets of particles.

Jet of particles

Quark

Proton

In the dense quark-gluon medium, the jets are quenched, like bullets fired into water, and on average only single jets emerge.

Quark-gluon medium

### Elliptic Flow
Off-center collisions between gold nuclei produce an elliptical region of quark-gluon medium.

Fragment of gold nucleus

Elliptical quark-gluon medium

The pressure gradients in the elliptical region cause it to explode outward, mostly in the plane of the collision (*arrows*) these hadrons formed were behaving collectively, before reverting back into hadrons. They were acting like a liquid—that is, not a gas. From a gas, the hadrons would emerge uniformly in all directions.

This liquid behavior of the quark-gluon medium must mean that these particles interact with one another rather strongly during their heady moments of liberation right after formation. The decrease in the strength of their interactions (caused by the asymptotic freedom of QCD) is apparently overwhelmed by a dramatic increase in the *number* of newly liberated particles. It is as though our poor prisoners have broken out of their cells, only to find themselves haplessly caught up in a jail-yard crush, jostling with all the other escapees. The resulting tightly coupled dance is exactly what happens in a liquid. This situation conflicts with the naive theoretical picture originally painted of this medium as an almost ideal, weakly interacting gas. And the detailed features of the elliptical asymmetry suggest that this surprising liquid flows with almost no viscosity. It is probably the most perfect liquid ever observed.

## The Emerging Theoretical Picture

Calculating the strong interactions occurring in a liquid of quarks and gluons that are squeezed to almost unimaginable densities and exploding outward at nearly the speed of light is an immense challenge. One approach is to perform brute-force solutions of QCD using huge arrays of microprocessors specially designed for this problem. In this so-called lattice-QCD approach, space is approximated by a discrete lattice of points (imagine a Tinkertoy structure). The QCD equations are solved by successive approximations on the lattice.

Using this technique, theorists have calculated such properties as pressure and energy density as a function of temperature; each of these dramatically increases when hadrons are transformed into a quark-gluon medium. But this method is best suited for static problems in which the medium is in thermodynamic equilibrium, unlike the rapidly changing conditions in RHIC's mini bangs. Even the most sophisticated lattice-QCD calculations have been unable to determine such dynamic features as jet quenching and viscosity. Although the viscosity of a system of strongly interacting particles is expected to be small, it cannot be exactly zero because of quantum mechanics. But answering the question "How low can it go?" has proved notoriously difficult.

Remarkably, help has arrived from an unexpected quarter: string theories of quantum gravity. An extraordinary conjecture by theorist Juan Maldacena of the Institute for Advanced Study in Princeton, N.J., has forged a surprising connection between a theory of strings in a warped five-dimensional space and a QCD-like theory of particles that exist on the four-dimensional boundary of that space [see "The Illusion of Gravity," by Juan Maldacena; *Scientific American*, November 2005].

The two theories are mathematically equivalent even though they appear to describe radically different realms of physics. When the QCD-like forces get strong, the corresponding string theory becomes weak and hence easier to evaluate. Quantities such as viscosity that are hard to calculate in QCD have counterparts in string theory (in this case, the absorption of gravity waves by a black hole) that are much more tractable. A very small but nonzero lower limit on what is called the specific viscosity emerges from this approach—only about a tenth of that of superfluid helium. Quite possibly, string theory may help us understand how quarks and gluons behaved during the earliest microseconds of the big bang.

## Future Challenges

Astonishingly, the hottest, densest matter ever encountered far exceeds all other known fluids in its approach to perfection. How and why this happens is the great experimental challenge now facing physicists at RHIC. The wealth of data from these experiments is already forcing theorists to reconsider some cherished ideas about matter in the early universe. In the past, most calculations treated the freed quarks and gluons as an ideal gas instead of a liquid. The theory of QCD and asymptotic freedom are not in any danger—no evidence exists to dispute the fundamental equations. What is up for debate are the techniques and simplifying assumptions used by theorists to draw conclusions from the equations.

To address these questions, experimenters are studying the different kinds of quarks emerging from the mini bangs, especially the heavier varieties. When quarks were originally predicted in 1964, they were thought to occur in three versions: up, down and strange. With masses below 0.15 GeV, these three species of quarks and their antiquarks are created copiously and in roughly equal numbers in RHIC collisions. Two additional quarks, dubbed charm and bottom, turned up in the 1970s, sporting much greater masses of about 1.6 and 5 GeV, respectively. Because much more energy is required to create these heavy quarks (according to $E = mc^2$), they appear earlier in the mini bangs (when energy densities are higher) and much less often. This rarity makes them valuable tracers of the flow patterns and other properties that develop early in the evolution of a mini bang.

The PHENIX and STAR experiments are well suited for such detailed studies because they can detect high-energy electrons and other particles called muons that often emerge from decays of these heavy quarks. Physicists then trace these and other decay particles back to their points of origin, providing crucial information about the heavy quarks that spawned them. With their greater masses, heavy quarks can have different flow patterns and behavior than their far more abundant cousins. Measuring these differences should help tease out precise values for the tiny residual viscosity anticipated.

Charm quarks have another characteristic useful for probing the quark-gluon medium. Usually about 1 percent of them are produced in a tight embrace with a charm antiquark, forming a neutral particle called the J/psi. The separation between the two partners is only about a third the radius of a proton, so the rate of J/psi production should be sensitive to the force between quarks at short distances. Theorists expect this force to fall off because the surrounding swarm of light quarks and gluons will tend to screen the charm quark and antiquark from each other, leading to less J/psi production. Recent PHENIX results indicate that J/psi particles do indeed dissolve in the fluid, similar to what was observed earlier at CERN, the European laboratory for particle physics near Geneva [see "Fireballs of Free Quarks," by Graham P. Collins, News and Analysis; *Scientific American*, April 2000]. Even greater J/psi suppression was expected to occur at RHIC because of the higher densities involved, but early results suggest some competing mechanism, such as reformation of J/psi particles, may occur at these densities. Further measurements will focus on this mystery by searching for other pairs of heavy quarks and observing whether and how their production is suppressed.

Another approach being pursued is to try to view the quark-gluon fluid by its own light. A hot broth of these particles should shine briefly, like the flash of a lightning bolt, because it emits high-energy photons that escape the medium unscathed. Just as astronomers measure the temperature of a distant star from its spectrum of light emission, physicists are trying to employ these energetic photons to determine the temperature of the quark-gluon fluid. But measuring this spectrum has thus far proved enormously challenging because many other photons are generated by the decay of hadrons called neutral pions. Although those photons are produced long after the quark-gluon fluid has reverted to hadrons, they all look the same when they arrive at the detectors.

Many physicists are now preparing for the next energy frontier at the Large Hadron Collider (LHC) at CERN. Starting in 2008, experiments there will observe collisions of lead nuclei at combined energies exceeding one million GeV. An international team of more than 1,000 physicists is building the mammoth ALICE detector, which will combine the capabilities of the PHENIX and STAR detectors in a single experiment. The mini bangs produced by the LHC will briefly reach several times the energy density that occurs in RHIC collisions, and the temperatures reached therein should easily surpass 10 trillion degrees. Physicists will then be able to simulate and study conditions that occurred during the very first microsecond of the big bang.

The overriding question is whether the liquidlike behavior witnessed at RHIC will persist at the higher temperatures and densities encountered at the LHC. Some theorists project that the force between quarks will become weak once their average energy exceeds 1 GeV, which will occur at the LHC, and that the quark-gluon plasma will finally start behaving properly—like a gas, as originally expected. Others are less sanguine. They maintain that the QCD force cannot fall off fast enough at these higher energies, so the quarks and gluons should remain tightly coupled in their liquid embrace. On this issue, we must await the verdict of experiment, which may well bring other surprises.

## More to Explore

**The Relativistic Heavy-Ion Collider: Creating a Little Big Bang on Long Island.** Frank Wolfs in *Beam Line*, pages 2–8; Spring/Summer 2001. Online at **www.slac.stanford.edu/pubs/beamline.**

**What Have We Learned from the Relativistic Heavy Ion Collider?** Thomas Ludlam and Larry McLerran in *Physics Today*, Vol. 56, No. 10, pages 48–54; October 2003.

RHIC home page: **www.bnl.gov/RHIC.**

RHIC animations: **www.phenix.bnl.gov/WWW/ software/luxor/ani.**

Web sites of the RHIC collaborations, which include links to research papers: **www.rhic.bnl.gov/brahms; www.phenix.bnl.gov; www.phobos.bnl.gov; and www.star.bnl.gov.**

## About the Authors

*MICHAEL RIORDAN* teaches the history of physics at Stanford University and at the University of California, Santa Cruz, where he is adjunct professor of physics. He is author of *The Hunting of the Quark* and co-author of *The Shadows of Creation*.

*WILLIAM A. ZAJC* is professor of physics at Columbia University. For the past eight years, he has served as scientific spokesperson for the PHENIX Experiment at RHIC, an international collaboration of more than 400 scientists from 13 nations.

# "An Echo of
## 2. Black Holes"

By Theodore A. Jacobson and Renaud Parentani

*Sound waves in a fluid behave uncannily like light waves in space. Black holes even have acoustic counterparts. Could spacetime literally be a kind of fluid, like the ether of pre-Einsteinian physics?*

When Albert Einstein proposed his special theory of relativity in 1905, he rejected the 19th-century idea that light arises from vibrations of a hypothetical medium, the "ether." Instead, he argued, light waves can travel in vacuo without being supported by any material—unlike sound waves, which are vibrations of the medium in which they propagate. This feature of special relativity is untouched in the two other pillars of modern physics, general relativity and quantum mechanics. Right up to the present day, all experimental data, on scales ranging from subnuclear to galactic, are successfully explained by these three theories.

Nevertheless, physicists face a deep conceptual problem. As currently understood, general relativity and quantum mechanics are incompatible. Gravity, which general relativity attributes to the curvature of the space-time continuum, stubbornly resists being incorporated into a quantum framework. Theorists have made only incremental progress toward understanding the highly curved structure of spacetime that quantum mechanics leads them to expect at extremely short distances.

## Overview/Acoustic Black Holes

- The famous physicist Stephen W. Hawking argued in the 1970s that black holes are not truly black; they emit a quantum glow of thermal radiation. But his analysis had a problem. According to relativity theory, waves starting at a black hole horizon will be stretched by an infinite amount as they propagate away. Therefore, Hawking's radiation must emerge from an infinitely small region of space, where the unknown effects of quantum gravity take over.

- Physicists have grappled with this problem by studying black hole analogues in fluid systems. The fluid's molecular structure cuts off the infinite stretching and replaces the microscopic mysteries of spacetime by known physics.

- The analogies lend credence to Hawking's conclusion. They also suggest to some researchers that spacetime has a "molecular" structure, contrary to the assumptions of standard relativity theory.

Frustrated, some have turned to an unexpected source for guidance: condensed-matter physics, the study of common substances such as crystals and fluids.

Like spacetime, condensed matter looks like a continuum when viewed at large scales, but unlike spacetime it has a well-understood microscopic structure governed by quantum mechanics. Moreover, the propagation of sound in an uneven fluid flow is closely analogous to the propagation of light in a curved spacetime. By studying a model of a black hole using sound waves, we and our colleagues are attempting to exploit this analogy to gain insight into the possible microscopic workings of spacetime. The work suggests that spacetime may, like a material fluid, be granular and possess a preferred frame of reference that manifests itself on fine scales—contrary to Einstein's assumptions.

# From Black Hole to Hot Coal

Black holes are a favorite testing ground for quantum gravity because they are among the few places where quantum mechanics and general relativity are both critically important. A major step toward a merger of the two theories came in 1974, when Stephen W. Hawking of the University of Cambridge applied quantum mechanics to the horizon of black holes.

According to general relativity, the horizon is the surface that separates the inside of a black hole (where gravity is so strong that nothing can escape) from the outside. It is not a material limit; unfortunate travelers falling into the hole would not sense anything special on crossing the horizon. But once having done so, they would no longer be able to send light signals to people outside, let alone return there. An outside observer would receive only the signals transmitted by the travelers before they crossed over. As light waves climb out of the gravitational well around a black hole, they get stretched out, shifting down in frequency and lengthening in duration. Consequently, to the observer, the travelers would appear to move in slow motion and to be redder than usual.

This effect, known as gravitational redshift, is not specific to black holes. It also alters the frequency and timing of signals between, say, orbiting satellites and ground stations. GPS navigation systems must take it into account to work accurately. What is specific to black holes, however, is that the redshift becomes infinite as the travelers approach the horizon. From the outside observer's point of view, the descent appears to take an infinite amount of time, even though only a finite time passes for the travelers themselves.

So far this description of black holes has treated light as a classical electromagnetic wave. What Hawking did was to reconsider the implications of the infinite redshift when the quantum nature of light is taken into account. According to quantum theory, even a perfect vacuum is not truly empty; it is filled with fluctuations as a result of the Heisenberg uncertainty principle. The fluctuations take the form of pairs of virtual photons. These photons are called virtual because, in an uncurved spacetime, far from any gravitational influence, they appear and disappear restlessly, remaining unobservable in the absence of any disturbance.

But in the curved spacetime around a black hole, one member of the pair can be trapped inside the horizon, while the other gets stranded outside. The pair can then pass from virtual to real, leading to an outward flux of observable light and a corresponding decrease in the mass of the hole. The overall pattern of radiation is thermal, like that from a hot coal, with a temperature inversely proportional to the mass of the black hole. This phenomenon is called the Hawking effect. Unless the hole swallows matter or energy to make up the loss, the Hawking radiation will drain it of all its mass.

An important point—which will become critical later when considering fluid analogies to black holes— is that the space very near the black hole horizon remains a nearly perfect quantum vacuum. In fact, this condition is essential for Hawking's argument. The virtual photons are a feature of the lowest-energy quantum state, or "ground state." It is only in the process of separating from their partners and climbing away from the horizon that the virtual photons become real.

## The Ultimate Microscope

Hawking's analysis has played a central role in the attempt to build a full quantum theory of gravity. The ability to reproduce and elucidate the effect is a crucial test for candidate quantum gravity theories, such as string theory [see "The Illusion of Gravity," by Juan Maldacena; *Scientific American*, November 2005]. Yet although most physicists accept Hawking's argument, they have never been able to confirm it experimentally. The predicted emission from stellar and galactic black holes is far too feeble to see. The only hope for observing Hawking radiation is to find miniature holes left over from the early universe or created in particle accelerators, which may well prove impossible [see "Quantum Black Holes," by Bernard Carr and Steven Giddings; *Scientific American*, May 2005].

The lack of empirical confirmation of the Hawking effect is particularly vexing in view of the disturbing fact that the theory has potential flaws, stemming from the infinite redshift that it predicts a photon will undergo. Consider what the emission process looks like when viewed reversed in time. As the Hawking photon gets

## Was Hawking Wrong?

One of the greatest—and least recognized—mysteries of black holes concerns a flaw in Stephen W. Hawking's famous prediction that black holes emit radiation. A hole is defined by an event horizon, a one-way door: objects on the outside can fall in, but objects on the inside cannot get out. Hawking asked what happens to pairs of virtual particles (which continually appear and disappear everywhere in empty space because of quantum effects) that originate at the horizon itself.

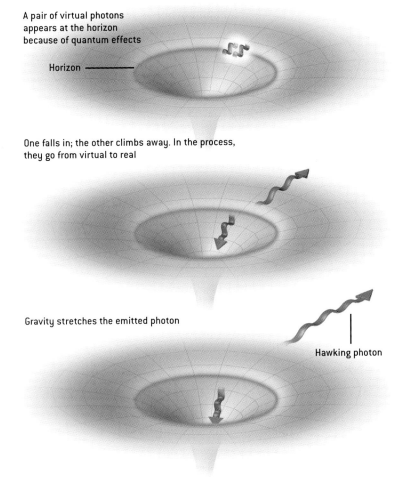

**A pair of virtual photons appears at the horizon because of quantum effects**

Horizon ————

**One falls in; the other climbs away. In the process, they go from virtual to real**

**Gravity stretches the emitted photon**

Hawking photon

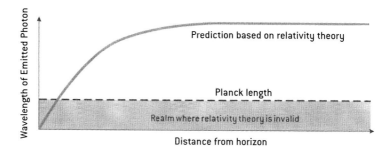

Relativity theory predicts that a photon from the horizon gets stretched by an infinite amount (*curve, above*). In other words, an observed photon must have originated as a virtual one with a wavelength of almost precisely zero, which is problematic because unknown quantum gravity effects take over at distances shorter than the so-called Planck length of $10^{-35}$ meter. This conundrum has driven physicists to design experimentally realizable analogues to black holes to see whether they indeed emit radiation and to understand how it originates.

nearer to the hole, it blueshifts to a higher frequency and correspondingly shorter wavelength. The further back in time it is followed, the closer it approaches the horizon and the shorter its wavelength becomes. Once the wavelength becomes much smaller than the black hole, the particle joins its partner and becomes the virtual pair discussed earlier.

The blueshifting continues without abatement, down to arbitrarily short distances. Smaller than a distance of about $10^{-35}$ meter, known as the Planck length, neither relativity nor standard quantum theory can predict what the particle will do. A quantum theory of gravity is needed. A black hole horizon thus acts as a fantastic microscope that brings the observer into contact with unknown physics. For a theorist, this magnification is worrisome. If Hawking's prediction relies on unknown physics, should we not be suspicious of its validity? Might the properties, even the existence, of Hawking radiation depend on the microscopic properties of spacetime—much as, for example, the heat capacity or speed of sound of a substance depends on its microscopic structure and dynamics? Or is the effect, as Hawking originally argued, entirely determined just by the macroscopic properties of the black hole, namely, its mass and spin?

## Sound Bites

One effort to answer these embarrassing questions began with the work of William Unruh of the University of British Columbia. In 1981 he showed that there is a close analogy between the propagation of sound in a moving fluid and that of light in a curved spacetime. He suggested that this analogy might be useful in assessing the impact of microscopic physics on the origin of Hawking radiation. Moreover, it might even allow for experimental observation of a Hawking-like phenomenon.

Like light waves, acoustic (sound) waves are characterized by a frequency, wavelength and propagation speed. The very concept of a sound wave is valid only when the wavelength is much longer than the distance between molecules of the fluid; on smaller scales, acoustic waves cease to exist. It is precisely this limitation that makes the analogy so interesting, because it can allow physicists to study the macroscopic consequences of microscopic structure. To be truly useful, however, this analogy must extend to the quantum level. Ordinarily, random thermal jigging of the molecules prevents sound waves from behaving analogously to light quanta. But when the temperature approaches absolute zero, sound can behave like quantum particles, which physicists call "phonons" to underline the analogy with the particles of light, photons. Experimenters routinely observe phonons in crystals and in substances that remain fluid at sufficiently low temperatures, such as liquid helium.

The behavior of phonons in a fluid at rest or moving uniformly is like that of photons in flat spacetime, where gravity is absent. Such phonons propagate in straight lines with unchanging wavelength, frequency and velocity. Sound in, say, a swimming pool or a smoothly flowing river travels straight from its source to the ear.

In a fluid moving nonuniformly, however, the phonons' velocity is altered and their wavelength can become stretched, just like photons in a curved space-time. Sound in a river entering a narrow canyon or water swirling down the drain becomes distorted and follows a bent path, like light around a star. In fact, the situation can be described using the geometrical tools of general relativity.

A fluid flow can even act on sound as a black hole acts on light. One way to create such an acoustic

## Light vs. Sound

| Type of wave | Classical description | Quantum description |
|---|---|---|
| Light | Oscillating electric and magnetic fields | Electromagnetic-wave photon |
| Sound | Collective movements of molecules | Acoustic-wave phonon |

black hole is to use a device that hydrodynamicists call a Laval nozzle. The nozzle is designed so that the fluid reaches and exceeds the speed of sound at the narrowest point without producing a shock wave (an abrupt change in fluid properties). The effective acoustic geometry is very similar to the spacetime geometry of a black hole. The supersonic region corresponds to the hole's interior: sound waves propagating against the direction of the flow are swept downstream, like light pulled toward the center of a hole. The subsonic region is the exterior of the hole: Sound waves can propagate upstream but only at the expense of being stretched, like light being redshifted. The boundary between the two regions behaves exactly like a black hole horizon.

## Atomism

If the fluid is cold enough, the analogy extends to the quantum level. Unruh argued that the sonic

| Velocity | What causes path of wave to curve | Where description breaks down |
|---|---|---|
| 300,000 kilometers per second | Spacetime curvature, caused by matter and energy | Planck length? ($10^{-35}$ meter) |
| 1,500 meters per second (in liquid water) | Variations in fluid speed and direction | Intermolecular distance ($10^{-10}$ meter for water) |

horizon emits thermal phonons analogous to Hawking radiation. Quantum fluctuations near the horizon cause pairs of phonons to appear; one partner gets swept into the supersonic region, never to return, while the other ripples upstream, getting stretched out by the fluid flow. A microphone placed upstream picks up a faint hiss. The sound energy of the hiss is drawn from the kinetic energy of the fluid flow.

The dominant tone of the noise depends on the geometry; the typical wavelength of the observed phonons is comparable to the distance over which the flow velocity changes appreciably. This distance is much larger than the distance between molecules, so Unruh did his original analysis assuming that the fluid is smooth and continuous. Yet the phonons originate near the horizon with wavelengths so short that they should be sensitive to the granularity of the fluid. Does that affect the end result? Does a real fluid emit Hawking-like phonons, or is Unruh's prediction an artifact of the idealization of a continuous fluid? If that question can be answered for acoustic black holes, it may by analogy guide physicists in the case of gravitational black holes.

Physicists have proposed a number of black hole analogues besides the transsonic fluid flow. One involves not sound waves but ripples on the surface of a liquid or along the interface between layers of superfluid helium, which is so cold that it has lost all frictional resistance to motion. Recently Unruh and Ralf Schützhold of the Technical University of Dresden in Germany proposed to study electromagnetic waves passing through a tiny, carefully engineered electronic pipe. By sweeping a laser along the pipe to change the local wave speed, physicists might be able to create a horizon. Yet another idea is to model the accelerating expansion of the universe, which generates a Hawking-like radiation. A Bose-Einstein condensate—a gas so cold that the atoms have lost their individual identity—can act on sound like an expanding universe does on light, either by literally flying apart or by being manipulated using a magnetic field to give the same effect.

As yet, experimenters have not created any of these devices in the laboratory. The procedures are complicated, and experimenters have plenty of other low-temperature phenomena to keep them busy. So theorists have been working to see whether they can make headway on the problem mathematically.

Understanding how the molecular structure of the fluid affects phonons is extremely complicated. Fortunately, 10 years after Unruh proposed his sonic analogy, one of us (Jacobson) came up with a very useful simplification. The essential details of the molecular structure are encapsulated in the way that the frequency of a sound wave depends on its wavelength. This dependence, called the dispersion relation, determines the velocity of propagation. For large wavelengths, the velocity is constant. For short wavelengths, approaching the intermolecular distance, the velocity can vary with wavelength.

Three different behaviors can arise. Type I is no dispersion—the wave behaves the same at short wavelengths as it does at long ones. For type II, the velocity decreases as the wavelength decreases, and for type III, velocity increases. Type I describes photons in relativity. Type II describes phonons in, for example, superfluid helium, and type III describes phonons in dilute Bose-Einstein condensates. This division into three types provides an organizing principle for figuring out how molecular structure affects sound on a macroscopic level. Beginning in 1995, Unruh and then other researchers have examined the Hawking effect in the presence of type II and type III dispersion.

Consider how the Hawking-like phonons look when viewed backward in time. Initially the dispersion type does not matter. The phonons swim downstream toward the horizon, their wavelengths decreasing all the while. Once the wavelength approaches the intermolecular distance, the specific dispersion relation becomes important. For type II, the phonons slow down, then reverse direction and start heading

## Black Hole Analogue

A Laval nozzle—found at the end of rockets—makes a ready analogue to a black hole. The incoming fluid is subsonic; the constriction forces it to accelerate to the speed of sound, so that the outgoing fluid is supersonic. Sound waves in the subsonic region can move upstream, whereas waves in the supersonic region cannot. The constriction thus acts just like the horizon of a black hole: sound can enter but not exit the supersonic region. Quantum fluctuations in the constriction should generate sound analogous to Hawking radiation.

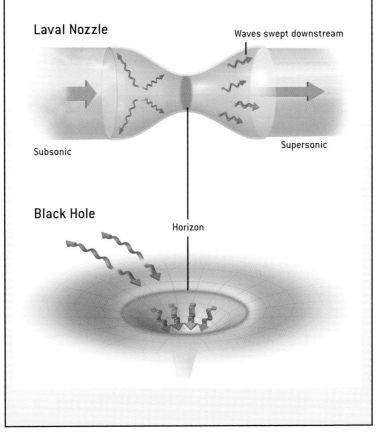

**Laval Nozzle**

Waves swept downstream

Subsonic

Supersonic

**Black Hole**

Horizon

upstream again. For type III, they accelerate, break the long-wavelength speed of sound, then cross the horizon.

## Ether Redux

A true analogy to the Hawking effect must meet an important condition: the virtual phonon pairs must begin life in their ground state, as do the virtual photon pairs around the black hole. In a real fluid, this condition would be easily met. As long as the macroscopic fluid flow changes slowly in time and space (compared with the pace of events at the molecular level), the molecular state continuously adjusts to minimize the energy of the system as a whole. It does not matter which molecules the fluid is made of.

With this condition met, it turns out that the fluid emits Hawking-like radiation no matter which of the three types of dispersion relations applies. The microscopic details of the fluid do not have any effect. They get washed out as the phonons travel away from the horizon. In addition, the arbitrarily short wavelengths invoked by original Hawking analysis do not arise when either type II or III dispersion is included. Instead the wavelengths bottom out at the intermolecular distance. The infinite redshift is an avatar of the unphysical assumption of infinitely small atoms.

Applied to real black holes, the fluid analogy lends confidence that Hawking's result is correct despite the

## Other Black Hole Models

Devices besides the Laval nozzle also reproduce the essential characteristic of a black hole horizon: waves can go one way but not the other. Each offers novel insights into black holes. All should generate the analogue of Hawking radiation.

### Surface Ripples

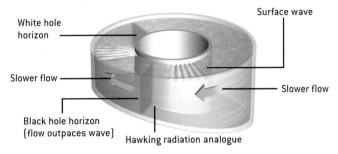

White hole horizon

Surface wave

Slower flow

Slower flow

Black hole horizon (flow outpaces wave)

Hawking radiation analogue

Instead of sound waves, this experiment involves surface waves in liquid flowing around a circular channel. As the channel becomes shallower, the flow speeds up and, at some point, outpaces the waves, preventing them from traveling upstream—thereby creating the analogue of a black hole horizon. Completing the circuit is the horizon of a "white hole": a body that lets material flow out but not in. To observe Hawking-like radiation would require a supercooled fluid such as helium 4.

### Electromagnetic-wave pipe

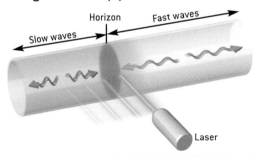

Horizon

Fast waves

Slow waves

Laser

This experiment studies microwaves passing through a rod built so that the speed of wave propagation can be tweaked with a laser beam. Sweeping the beam along the rod creates a moving horizon that divides the rod into slow- and fast-wave zones. Waves in the slow zone cannot reach the fast zone, but waves in the fast zone can cross to the slow. The Hawking-like radiation may be stronger and easier to observe than in fluid analogies.

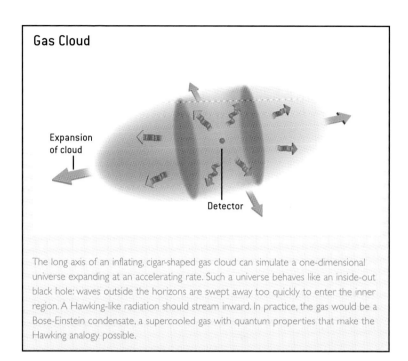

**Gas Cloud**

Expansion of cloud

Detector

The long axis of an inflating, cigar-shaped gas cloud can simulate a one-dimensional universe expanding at an accelerating rate. Such a universe behaves like an inside-out black hole: waves outside the horizons are swept away too quickly to enter the inner region. A Hawking-like radiation should stream inward. In practice, the gas would be a Bose-Einstein condensate, a supercooled gas with quantum properties that make the Hawking analogy possible.

simplifications he made. Moreover, it suggests to some researchers that the infinite redshift at a gravitational black hole horizon may be similarly avoided by dispersion of short wavelength light. But there is a catch. Relativity theory flatly asserts that light does not undergo dispersion in a vacuum. The wavelength of a photon appears different to different observers; it is arbitrarily long when viewed from a reference frame that is moving sufficiently close to the speed of light. Hence, the laws of physics cannot mandate a fixed short-wavelength cutoff, at which the dispersion relation changes from type I to type II or III. Each observer would perceive a different cutoff.

## Hawking Was Right, But . . .

The fluid analogies suggest how to fix Hawking's analysis. In an idealized fluid, the speed of sound is the same no matter the wavelength (so-called type I behavior). In a real fluid, the speed of sound either decreases (type II) or increases (type III) as the wavelength approaches the distance between molecules.

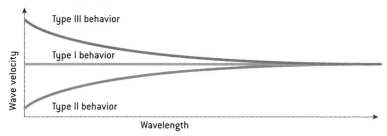

Hawking's analysis is based on standard relativity theory, in which light travels at a constant speed—type I behavior. If its speed varied with wavelength, as in the fluid analogues, the paths of the Hawking photons would change.

For type II, the photons originate outside the horizon and fall inward. One undergoes a shift of velocity, reverses course and flies out.

For type III, the photons originate inside the horizon. One accelerates past the usual speed of light, allowing it to escape.

Because the photons do not originate exactly at the horizon, they do not become infinitely redshifted. This fix to Hawking's analysis has a price: relativity theory must be modified. Contrary to Einstein's assumptions, spacetime must act like a fluid consisting of some unknown kind of "molecules."

Physicists thus face a dilemma. Either they retain Einstein's injunction against a preferred frame and they swallow the infinite redshifting, or they assume that photons do not undergo an infinite redshift and they have to introduce a preferred reference frame. Would this frame necessarily violate relativity? No one yet knows. Perhaps the preferred frame is a local effect that arises only near black hole horizons—in which case relativity continues to apply in general. On the other hand, perhaps the preferred frame exists every-where, not just near black holes—in which case relativity is merely an approximation to a deeper theory of nature. Experimenters have yet to see such a frame, but the null result may simply be for want of sufficient precision.

Physicists have long suspected that reconciling general relativity with quantum mechanics would involve a short-distance cutoff, probably related to the Planck scale. The acoustic analogy bolsters this suspicion. Spacetime must be somehow granular to tame the dubious infinite redshift.

If so, the analogy between sound and light propa-gation would be even better than Unruh originally thought. The unification of general relativity and quantum mechanics may lead us to abandon the idealization of continuous space and time and to dis-cover the "atoms" of spacetime. Einstein may have had similar thoughts when he wrote to his close friend Michele Besso in 1954, the year before his death: "I consider it quite possible that physics cannot be based on the field concept, that is, on continuous structures."

But this would knock out the very foundation from under physics, and at present scientists have no clear candidate for a substitute. Indeed, Einstein went on to say in his next sentence, "Then *nothing* remains of my entire castle in the air, including the theory of gravitation, but also nothing of the rest of modern physics." Fifty years later the castle remains intact, although its future is unclear. Black holes and their acoustic analogues have perhaps begun to light the path and sound out the way.

## More to Explore

**Trans-Planckian Redshifts and the Substance of the Space-Time River.** Ted Jacobson in *Progress of Theoretical Physics Supplement*, No. 136, pages 1–17; 1999. Available (free registration) at **http://ptp.ipap.jp/cgi-bin/getarticle?magazine= PTPS&volume=136&number=&page=1-17.**

**What Did We Learn from Studying Acoustic Black Holes?** Renaud Parentani in *International Journal of Modern Physics A*, Vol. 17, No. 20, pages 2721–2726; August 10, 2002. Preprint available at **http://arxiv.org/abs/gr-qc/0204079.**

**Black-Hole Physics in an Electromagnetic Waveguide.** Steven K. Blau in *Physics Today*, Vol. 58, No. 8, pages 19–20; August 2005.

For papers presented at the workshop on "Analog Models of General Relativity," see **www.physics.wustl.edu/?visser/Analog.**

## About the Authors

*THEODORE A. JACOBSON* and *RENAUD PARENTANI* study the puzzles of quantum gravity and its possible observable consequences for black holes and cosmology. Jacobson is a physics professor at the University of Maryland. His recent research focuses on the thermodynamics of black holes, how spacetime might be microscopically discrete and whether that fine structure could be macroscopically detected. Parentani is a physics professor at the University of Paris–Sud at Orsay who does research at the CNRS Laboratory of Theoretical Physics. He investigates the role of quantum fluctuations in black hole physics and cosmology. This article is a translation and update of Parentani's article in the May 2002 issue of *Pour la Science*, the French edition of *Scientific American*.

# "The Illusion
3. of Gravity"

By Juan Maldacena

*The force of gravity and one of the dimensions of space might be generated out of the peculiar interactions of particles and fields existing in a lower-dimensional realm.*

Three spatial dimensions are visible all around us—up/down, left/right, forward/backward. Add time to the mix, and the result is a four-dimensional blending of space and time known as spacetime. Thus, we live in a four-dimensional universe. Or do we?

Amazingly, some new theories of physics predict that one of the three dimensions of space could be a kind of an illusion—that in actuality all the particles and fields that make up reality are moving about in a two-dimensional realm like the Flatland of Edwin A. Abbott. Gravity, too, would be part of the illusion: a force that is not present in the two-dimensional world but that materializes along with the emergence of the illusory third dimension.

Or, more precisely, the theories predict that the number of dimensions in reality could be a matter of perspective: physicists could choose to describe reality as obeying one set of laws (including gravity) in three dimensions or, equivalently, as obeying a different set of laws that operates in two dimensions (in the absence of gravity). Despite the radically different descriptions, both theories would describe everything that we see and

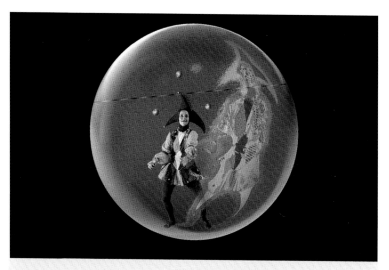

Holographic theory relates one set of physical laws acting in a volume with a different set of physical laws acting on a boundary surface, as represented here by the juggler and her colorful two-dimensional image. The surface laws involve quantum particles that have "color" charges and interact very like the quarks and gluons of standard particle physics. The interior laws are a form of string theory and include the force of gravity (experienced by the juggler), which is hard to describe in terms of quantum mechanics. Nevertheless, the physics on the surface and in the interior are completely equivalent, despite their radically different descriptions.

all the data we could gather about how the universe works. We would have no way to determine which theory was "really" true.

Such a scenario strains the imagination. Yet an analogous phenomenon occurs in everyday life. A hologram is a two-dimensional object, but when viewed under the correct lighting conditions it produces a fully three-dimensional image. All the information describing the three-dimensional image is in essence encoded in the two-dimensional hologram. Similarly, according to the new physics theories, the entire universe could be a kind of a hologram [see "Information in the Holographic Universe," by Jacob D. Bekenstein; *Scientific American*, August 2003].

The holographic description is more than just an intellectual or philosophical curiosity. A computation that might be very difficult in one realm can turn out to be relatively straightforward in the other, thereby turning some intractable problems of physics into ones that are easily solved. For example, the theory seems useful in analyzing a recent experimental high-energy physics result. Moreover, the holographic theories offer a fresh way to begin constructing a quantum theory of gravity—a theory of gravity that respects the principles of quantum mechanics. A quantum theory of gravity is a key ingredient in any effort to unify all the forces of nature, and it is needed to explain both what goes on in black holes and what happened in the nanoseconds after the big bang. The holographic theories provide potential resolutions of profound mysteries that have dogged attempts to understand how a theory of quantum gravity could work.

## A Difficult Marriage

A quantum theory of gravity is a holy grail for a certain breed of physicist because all physics except for gravity is well described by quantum laws. The quantum description of physics represents an entire paradigm for physical theories, and it makes no sense for one theory, gravity, to fail to conform to it. Now about 80 years old, quantum mechanics was first developed to describe the behavior of particles and forces in the atomic and sub-atomic realms. It is at those size scales that quantum effects become significant. In quantum theories, objects do not have definite positions and velocities but instead are described by probabilities and waves that occupy regions of space. In a quantum world, at the most fundamental level everything is in a state of constant flux, even "empty" space, which is in fact filled with virtual particles that perpetually pop in and out of existence.

In contrast, physicists' best theory of gravity, general relativity, is an inherently classical (that is, nonquantum)

## Overview/Equivalent Worlds

- According to a remarkable theory, a universe that exists in two dimensions and is without gravity may be completely equivalent to a three-dimensional universe with gravity. The three-dimensional universe would emerge from the physics of the two-dimensional universe somewhat like a holographic image arising from a hologram.

- The two-dimensional universe exists on the boundary of the three-dimensional universe. The physics on the boundary looks like strongly interacting quarks and gluons. The physics on the interior includes a quantum theory of gravity—something that string theorists have been developing for decades.

- The equivalence provides a new way to understand properties of black holes, which require a suitable melding of quantum mechanics and gravity. The mathematics of the theory has not yet been rigorously proved, but it seems useful in analyzing a recent experimental high-energy physics result.

theory. Einstein's magnum opus, general relativity explains that concentrations of matter or energy cause spacetime to curve and that this curvature deflects the trajectories of particles, just as should happen for particles in a gravitational field. General relativity is a beautiful theory, and many of its predictions have been tested to great accuracy.

In a classical theory such as general relativity, objects have definite locations and velocities, like the planets orbiting the sun. One can plug those locations and velocities (and the masses of the objects) into the equations of general relativity and deduce the curvature of spacetime and from that deduce the effects of gravity on the objects' trajectories. Furthermore, empty spacetime is perfectly smooth no matter how closely one examines it—a seamless arena in which matter and energy can play out their lives.

The problem in devising a quantum version of general relativity is not just that on the scale of atoms and electrons, particles do not have definite locations and velocities. To make matters worse, at the even tinier scale delineated by the Planck length ($10^{-33}$ centimeter), quantum principles imply that spacetime itself should be a seething foam, similar to the sea of virtual particles that fills empty space. When matter and spacetime are so protean, what do the equations of general relativity predict? The answer is that the equations are no longer adequate. If we assume that matter obeys the laws of quantum mechanics and gravity obeys the laws of general relativity, we end up with mathematical contradictions. A quantum theory of gravity (one that fits within the paradigm of quantum theories) is needed.

In most situations, the contradictory requirements of quantum mechanics and general relativity are not a problem, because either the quantum effects or the gravitational effects are so small that they can be neglected or dealt with by approximations. When the curvature of spacetime is very large, however, the quantum aspects of gravity become significant. It takes a very large mass or a great concentration of mass to produce much spacetime curvature. Even the curvature produced near the sun is exceedingly small compared with the amount needed for quantum gravity effects to become apparent.

Though these effects are completely negligible now, they were very important in the beginning of the big bang, which is why a quantum theory of gravity is needed to describe how the big bang started. Such a theory is also important for understanding what happens at the center of black holes, because matter there is crushed into a region of extremely high curvature. Because gravity involves spacetime curvature, a quantum gravity theory will also be a theory of quantum space-time; it should clarify what constitutes the "spacetime foam" mentioned earlier, and it will probably provide us with an entirely new perspective on what spacetime is at the deepest level of reality.

A very promising approach to a quantum theory of gravity is string theory, which some theoretical physicists have been exploring since the 1970s. String theory overcomes some of the obstacles to building a logically consistent quantum theory of gravity. String theory, however, is still under construction and is not yet fully understood. That is, we string theorists have some approximate equations for strings, but we do not know the exact equations. We also do not know the guiding underlying principle that explains the form of the equations, and there are innumerable physical quantities that we do not know how to compute from the equations.

In recent years string theorists have obtained many interesting and surprising results, giving novel ways of understanding what a quantum spacetime is like. I will not describe string theory in much detail here [see "The String Theory Landscape," by Raphael Bousso and Joseph Polchinski; *Scientific American*, September 2004] but instead will focus on one of the most exciting recent developments emerging from string theory research, which led to a complete, logically consistent, quantum description of gravity in what are called negatively curved spacetimes—the first such description ever developed. For these spacetimes, holographic theories appear to be true.

## Negatively Curved Spacetimes

All of us are familiar with Euclidean geometry, where space is flat (that is, not curved). It is the geometry of figures drawn on flat sheets of paper. To a very good approximation, it is also the geometry of the world around us: parallel lines never meet, and all the rest of Euclid's axioms hold.

We are also familiar with some curved spaces. Curvature comes in two forms, positive and negative. The simplest space with positive curvature is the surface of a sphere. A sphere has constant positive curvature. That is, it has the same degree of curvature at every location (unlike an egg, say, which has more curvature at the pointy end).

The simplest space with negative curvature is called hyperbolic space, which is defined as space with constant negative curvature. This kind of space has long fascinated scientists and artists alike. Indeed, M. C. Escher produced several beautiful pictures of hyperbolic space.

By including time in the game, physicists can similarly consider space*times* with positive or negative curvature. The simplest spacetime with positive curvature is called de Sitter space, after Willem de Sitter, the Dutch physicist who introduced it. Many cosmologists believe that the very early universe was close to being a de Sitter space. The far future may also be de Sitter–like because of cosmic acceleration. Conversely, the simplest negatively curved spacetime is called anti–de Sitter space. It is similar to hyperbolic space except that it also contains a time direction. Unlike our universe, which is expanding, anti–de Sitter space is neither expanding nor contracting. It looks the same at all times. Despite that difference, anti–de Sitter space turns out to be quite useful in the quest to form quantum theories of spacetime and gravity.

If we picture hyperbolic space as being a disk, then anti–de Sitter space is like a stack of those disks, forming a solid cylinder. Time runs along the cylinder. Hyperbolic space can have more than two spatial dimensions. The anti–de Sitter space most like our spacetime (with three spatial dimensions) would have a three-dimensional "Escher print" as the cross section of its "cylinder."

Physics in anti–de Sitter space has some strange properties. If you were freely floating anywhere in anti–de Sitter space, you would feel as though you were at the bottom of a gravitational well. Any object that you threw out would come back like a boomerang. Surprisingly, the time required for an object to come back would be independent of how hard you threw it. The difference would just be that the harder you threw it, the farther away it would get on its round-trip back to you. If you sent a flash of light, which consists of photons moving at the maximum possible speed (the speed of light), it would actually reach infinity and come back to you, all in a finite amount of time. This can happen because an object experiences a kind of time contraction of ever greater magnitude as it gets farther away from you.

## The Hologram

Anti–de sitter space, although it is infinite, has a "boundary," located out at infinity. To draw this boundary, physicists and mathematicians use a distorted length scale, squeezing an infinite distance into a finite one. This boundary is like the surface of the solid cylinder I considered earlier. In the cylinder example, the boundary has two dimensions—one is space (looping around the cylinder), and one is time (running along its length). For four-dimensional anti–de Sitter space, the boundary has two space dimensions and one time dimension. The boundary of four-dimensional anti–de Sitter space at any moment in time is a sphere. This boundary is where the hologram of the holographic theory lies.

Stated simply, the idea is as follows: a quantum gravity theory in the interior of an anti–de Sitter space-time is completely equivalent to an ordinary quantum particle theory living on the boundary. If true, this equivalence means that we can use a quantum particle theory (which is relatively well understood) to define a quantum gravity theory (which is not).

To make an analogy, imagine you have two copies of a movie, one on reels of 70-millimeter film and one on a DVD. The two formats are utterly different, the first a linear ribbon of celluloid with each frame recognizably related to scenes of the movie as we know it, the second a two-dimensional platter with rings of magnetized dots that would form a sequence of 0s and 1s if we could perceive them at all. Yet both "describe" the same movie.

Similarly, the two theories, superficially utterly different in content, describe the same universe. The DVD looks like a metal disk with some glints of rainbowlike patterns. The boundary particle theory "looks like" a theory of particles in the absence of gravity. From the DVD, detailed pictures emerge only when the bits are processed the right way. From the boundary particle theory, quantum gravity and an extra dimension emerge when the equations are analyzed the right way.

What does it really mean for the two theories to be equivalent? First, for every entity in one theory, the other theory has a counterpart. The entities may be very different in how they are described by the theories: one entity in the interior might be a single particle of some type, corresponding on the boundary to a whole collection of particles of another type, considered as one entity. Second, the predictions for corresponding entities must be identical. Thus, if two particles have a 40 percent chance of colliding in the interior, the two corresponding collections of particles on the boundary should also have a 40 percent chance of colliding.

Here is the equivalence in more detail. The particles that live on the boundary interact in a way that is very similar to how quarks and gluons interact in reality (quarks are the constituents of protons and neutrons; gluons generate the strong nuclear force that binds the quarks together). Quarks have a kind of charge that comes in three varieties, called colors, and the interaction is called chromodynamics. The difference between the boundary particles and ordinary quarks and gluons is that the particles have a large number of colors, not just three.

Gerard 't Hooft of Utrecht University in the Netherlands studied such theories as long ago as 1974 and predicted that the gluons would form chains that behave much like the strings of string theory. The precise nature of these strings remained elusive, but in 1981 Alexander M. Polyakov, now at Princeton University, noticed that the strings effectively live in a higher-dimensional space than the gluons do. As we shall see shortly, in our holographic theories that higher-dimensional space is the interior of anti–de Sitter space.

To understand where the extra dimension comes from, start by considering one of the gluon strings on the boundary. This string has a thickness, related to how much its gluons are smeared out in space. When physicists calculate how these strings on the boundary of anti–de Sitter space interact with one another, they get a very odd result: two strings with different thicknesses do not interact very much with each other. It is as though the strings were separated spatially. One can reinterpret the thickness of the string to be a new spatial coordinate that goes away from the boundary.

Thus, a thin boundary string is like a string close to the boundary, whereas a thick boundary string is like one far away from the boundary. The extra coordinate is precisely the coordinate needed to describe motion within the four-dimensional anti–de Sitter spacetime! From the perspective of an observer in the spacetime, boundary strings of different thicknesses appear to be strings (all of them thin) at different radial locations. The number of colors on the boundary determines the size of the interior. To have a spacetime as large as the visible universe, the theory must have about $10^{60}$ colors.

It turns out that one type of gluon chain behaves in the four-dimensional spacetime as the graviton, the fundamental quantum particle of gravity. In this description, gravity in four dimensions is an emergent phenomenon arising from particle interactions in a gravityless, three-dimensional world. The presence of gravitons in the theory should come as no surprise— physicists have known since 1974 that string theories always give rise to quantum gravity. The strings formed by gluons are no exception, but the gravity operates in the higher-dimensional space.

Thus, the holographic correspondence is not just a wild new possibility for a quantum theory of gravity. Rather, in a fundamental way, it connects string theory, the most studied approach to quantum gravity, with theories of quarks and gluons, which are the cornerstone of particle physics. What is more, the holographic theory seems to provide some insight into the elusive exact equations of string theory. String theory was actually invented in the late 1960s for the purpose of describing strong interactions, but it was later abandoned (for that purpose) when the theory of chromodynamics entered the scene. The correspondence between string theory and chromodynamics implies that these early efforts were not misguided; the two descriptions are different faces of the same coin.

Varying the boundary chromodynamics theory by changing the details of how the boundary particles interact gives rise to an assortment of interior theories. The resulting interior theory can have only gravitational forces, or gravity plus some extra force such as the electromagnetic force, and so on. Unfortunately, we do not yet know of a boundary theory that gives rise to an interior theory that includes exactly the four forces we have in our universe.

I first conjectured that this holographic correspondence might hold for a specific theory (a simplified chromodynamics in a four-dimensional boundary spacetime) in 1997. This immediately excited great interest from the string theory community. The conjecture was made more precise by Polyakov, Stephen S. Gubser and Igor R. Klebanov of Princeton and Edward Witten of the Institute for Advanced Study in Princeton, N.J. Since then, many researchers have contributed to exploring the conjecture and generalizing it to other dimensions and other chromodynamics theories, providing mounting evidence that it is correct. So far, however, no example has been rigorously proved—the mathematics is too difficult.

## Mysteries of Black Holes

How does the holographic description of gravity help to explain aspects of black holes? Black holes are predicted to emit Hawking radiation, named after Stephen W. Hawking of the University of Cambridge, who discovered this result. This radiation comes out of the black hole at a specific temperature. For all ordinary physical systems, a theory called statistical mechanics explains temperature in terms of the motion of the microscopic constituents. This theory explains the temperature of a glass of water or the temperature of the sun. What about the temperature of a black hole? To understand it, we would need to know what the microscopic constituents of the black hole are and how they behave. Only a theory of quantum gravity can tell us that.

Some aspects of the thermodynamics of black holes have raised doubts as to whether a quantum-mechanical theory of gravity could be developed at all. It seemed as if quantum mechanics itself might break down in the face of effects taking place in black holes. For a black hole in an anti–de Sitter spacetime, we now know that quantum mechanics remains intact, thanks to the boundary theory. Such a black hole corresponds to a configuration of particles on the boundary. The number of particles is very large, and they are all zipping around, so that theorists can apply the usual rules of statistical mechanics to compute the temperature. The result is the same as the temperature that Hawking computed by very different means, indicating that the results can be trusted. Most important, the boundary theory obeys the ordinary rules of quantum mechanics; no inconsistency arises.

## Understanding Black Holes

Physicist Stephen W. Hawking showed in the 1970s that black holes have a temperature and give off radiation, but physicists since then have been deeply puzzled. Temperature is a property of a collection of particles, but what is the collection that defines a black hole? The holographic theory solves this puzzle by showing that a black hole is equivalent to a swarm of interacting particles on the boundary surface of spacetime.

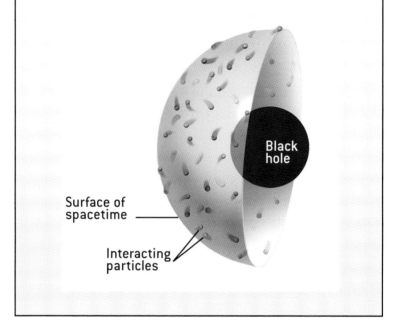

Black hole

Surface of spacetime ———

Interacting particles

Physicists have also used the holographic correspondence in the opposite direction—employing known properties of black holes in the interior spacetime to deduce the behavior of quarks and gluons at very high temperatures on the boundary. Dam Son of the University of Washington and his collaborators studied a quantity called the shear viscosity, which is small for a fluid that flows very easily and large for a substance more like molasses. They found that black holes have an extremely low shear viscosity—smaller than any known fluid. Because of the holographic equivalence, strongly interacting quarks and gluons at high temperatures should also have very low viscosity.

A test of this prediction comes from the Relativistic Heavy Ion Collider (RHIC) at Brookhaven National Laboratory, which has been colliding gold nuclei at very high energies. A preliminary analysis of these experiments indicates the collisions are creating a fluid with very low viscosity. Even though Son and his co-workers studied a simplified version of chromodynamics, they seem to have come up with a property that is shared by the real world. Does this mean that RHIC is creating small five-dimensional black holes? It is really too early to tell, both experimentally and theoretically. (Even if so, there is nothing to fear from these tiny black holes—they evaporate almost as fast as they are formed, and they "live" in five dimensions, not in our own four-dimensional world.)

Many questions about the holographic theories remain to be answered. In particular, does anything similar hold for a universe like ours in place of the anti–de Sitter space? A crucial aspect of anti–de Sitter space is that it has a boundary where time is well defined. The boundary has existed and will exist forever. An expanding universe, like ours, that comes from a big bang does not have such a well-behaved boundary. Consequently, it is not clear how to define a holographic theory for our universe; there is no convenient place to put the hologram.

An important lesson that one can draw from the holographic conjecture, however, is that quantum gravity, which has perplexed some of the best minds on the planet for decades, can be very simple when viewed in terms of the right variables. Let's hope we will soon find a simple description for the big bang!

## More to Explore

**Anti–de Sitter Space and Holography.** Edward Witten in Advances in *Theoretical and Mathematical Physics*, Vol. 2, pages 253–291; 1998. Available online at **http://arxiv.org/abs/hep-th/9802150.**

**Gauge Theory Correlators from Non-Critical String Theory.** S. Gubser, I. R. Klebanov and A. M. Polyakov in *Applied Physics Letters B*, Vol. 428, pages 105–114; 1998. **http://arxiv.org/abs/hep-th/9802109.**

**The Theory Formerly Known as Strings.** Michael J. Duff in *Scientific American*, Vol. 278, No. 2, pages 64–69; February 1998.

**The Elegant Universe.** Brian Greene. Reissue edition. W. W. Norton and Company, 2003.

A string theory Web site is at **superstringtheory.com.**

## About the Author

*JUAN MALDACENA* is a professor in the School of Natural Sciences at the Institute for Advanced Study in Princeton, N.J. Previously he was in the physics department at Harvard University from 1997 to 2001.

He is currently studying various aspects of the duality conjecture described in this article. String theorists were so impressed with the conjecture that at the Strings '98 conference they feted him with a song, "The Maldacena," sung and danced to the tune of "The Macarena."

# "The Mysteries
## 4. of Mass"

By Gordon Kane

*Physicists are hunting for an elusive particle that would reveal the presence of a new kind of field that permeates all of reality. Finding that Higgs field will give us a more complete understanding about how the universe works.*

Most people think they know what mass is, but they understand only part of the story. For instance, an elephant is clearly bulkier and weighs more than an ant. Even in the absence of gravity, the elephant would have greater mass—it would be harder to push and set in motion. Obviously the elephant is more massive because it is made of many more atoms than the ant is, but what determines the masses of the individual atoms? What about the elementary particles that make up the atoms—what determines their masses? Indeed, why do they even have mass?

We see that the problem of mass has two independent aspects. First, we need to learn how mass arises at all. It turns out mass results from at least three different mechanisms, which I will describe below. A key player in physicists' tentative theories about mass is a new kind of field that permeates all of reality, called the Higgs field. Elementary particle masses are thought to come about from the interaction with the Higgs field. If the Higgs field exists, theory demands that it have an associated particle, the Higgs

Male African elephant (about 6,000 kilograms) and the smallest species of ant (0.01 milligram) differ in mass by more than 11 orders of magnitude—roughly the same span as the top quark and the neutrino. Why the particle masses should differ by such a large amount remains a mystery.

boson. Using particle accelerators, scientists are now hunting for the Higgs.

The second aspect is that scientists want to know why different species of elementary particles have their specific quantities of mass. Their intrinsic masses span at least 11 orders of magnitude, but we do not yet know why that should be so [see "Male African Elephant" illustration]. For comparison, an elephant and the smallest of ants differ by about 11 orders of magnitude of mass.

## What Is Mass?

Isaac Newton presented the earliest scientific definition of mass in 1687 in his landmark *Principia*: "The quantity of matter is the measure of the same, arising from its density and bulk conjointly." That very basic definition was good enough for Newton and other scientists for more than 200 years. They understood that science should proceed first by describing how things work and later by understanding why. In recent years, however, the *why* of mass has become a research topic in physics. Understanding the meaning and origins of mass will complete and extend the Standard Model of particle physics, the well-established theory that describes the known elementary particles and their interactions. It will also resolve mysteries such as dark matter, which makes up about 25 percent of the universe.

The foundation of our modern understanding of mass is far more intricate than Newton's definition and is based on the Standard Model. At the heart of the Standard Model is a mathematical function called a Lagrangian, which represents how the various particles interact. From that function, by following rules known as relativistic quantum theory, physicists can calculate the behavior of the elementary particles, including how they come together to form compound particles, such as protons. For both the elementary particles and the compound ones, we can then calculate how they will respond to forces, and for a force $F$, we can write Newton's equation $F = ma$, which relates the force, the mass and the resulting acceleration. The Lagrangian tells us what to use for $m$ here, and that is what is meant by the mass of the particle.

But mass, as we ordinarily understand it, shows up in more than just $F = ma$. For example, Einstein's special relativity theory predicts that massless particles in a vacuum travel at the speed of light and that particles with mass travel more slowly, in a way that can be calculated if we know their mass. The laws of gravity predict that gravity acts on mass and energy as well, in a precise manner. The quantity $m$ deduced from the Lagrangian for each particle behaves correctly in all those ways, just as we expect for a given mass.

Fundamental particles have an intrinsic mass known as their rest mass (those with zero rest mass are called massless). For a compound particle, the constituents' rest mass and also their kinetic energy of motion and potential energy of interactions contribute to the particle's total mass. Energy and mass are related, as described by Einstein's famous equation, $E = mc^2$ (energy equals mass times the speed of light squared).

An example of energy contributing to mass occurs in the most familiar kind of matter in the universe— the protons and neutrons that make up atomic nuclei

## Overview/Higgs Physics

- Mass is a seemingly everyday property of matter, but it is actually mysterious to scientists in many ways. How do elementary particles acquire mass in the first place, and why do they have the specific masses that they do?

- The answers to those questions will help theorists complete and extend the Standard Model of particle physics, which describes the physics that governs the universe. The extended Standard Model may also help solve the puzzle of the invisible dark matter that accounts for about 25 percent of the cosmos.

- Theories say that elementary particles acquire mass by interacting with a quantum field that permeates all of reality. Experiments at particle accelerators may soon detect direct evidence of this so-called Higgs field.

in stars, planets, people and all that we see. These particles amount to 4 to 5 percent of the mass-energy of the universe [see "A Cosmic Stocktaking" box]. The Standard Model tells us that protons and neutrons are composed of elementary particles called quarks that are bound together by massless particles called gluons. Although the constituents are whirling around inside each proton, from outside we see a proton as a coherent object with an intrinsic mass, which is given by adding up the masses and energies of its constituents.

The Standard Model lets us calculate that nearly all the mass of protons and neutrons is from the kinetic energy of their constituent quarks and gluons (the remainder is from the quarks' rest mass). Thus, about 4 to 5 percent of the entire universe—almost all the familiar matter around us—comes from the energy of motion of quarks and gluons in protons and neutrons.

## Properties of the Elusive Higgs

### Permeating Reality

A typical field, such as the electromagnetic field, has its lowest energy at zero field strength (*left*). The universe is akin to a ball that rolled around and came to rest at the bottom of the valley—that is, it has settled at a field strength of zero. The Higgs, in contrast, has its minimum energy at a nonzero field strength, and the "ball" comes to rest at a nonzero value (*right*). Thus, the universe, in its natural lowest energy state, is permeated by that nonzero value of the Higgs field.

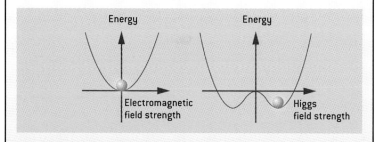

### Causing Two Phenomena

Two completely different phenomena—the acquisition of mass by a particle (*top*) and the production of a Higgs boson (*bottom*)—are caused by exactly the same interaction. This fact will be of great use in testing the Higgs theory by experiments.

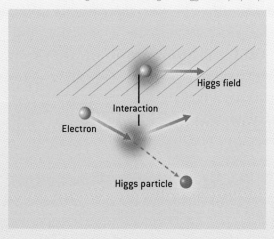

## Interacting with Other Particles

Force diagrams called Feynman diagrams represent how the Higgs particle interacts with other particles. Diagram (*a*) represents a particle such as a quark or an electron emitting (*shown*) or absorbing a Higgs particle. Diagram (*b*) shows the corresponding process for a W or Z boson. The W and Z can also interact simultaneously with two Higgs, as shown in (*c*), which also represents a W or Z scattering (roughly speaking, colliding with) a Higgs particle. The interactions represented by diagrams (*a*) through (*c*) are also responsible for generating particles' masses. The Higgs also interacts with itself, as represented by diagrams (*d*) and (*e*). More complicated processes can be built up by joining together copies of these elementary diagrams. Interactions depicted in (*d*) and (*e*) are responsible for the shape of the energy graph (*top, page 72*).

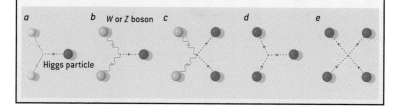

*a*  *b* W or Z boson  *c*  *d*  *e*

Higgs particle

# The Higgs Mechanism

Unlike protons and neutrons, truly elementary particles—such as quarks and electrons—are not made up of smaller pieces. The explanation of how they acquire their rest masses gets to the very heart of the problem of the origin of mass. As I noted above, the account proposed by contemporary theoretical physics is that fundamental particle masses arise from interactions with the Higgs field. But why is the Higgs field present throughout the universe? Why isn't its strength essentially zero on cosmic scales, like the electromagnetic field? What *is* the Higgs field?

The Higgs field is a quantum field. That may sound mysterious, but the fact is that all elementary particles arise as quanta of a corresponding quantum field. The electromagnetic field is also a quantum field (its corresponding elementary particle is the photon). So in this respect, the Higgs field is no more enigmatic than electrons and light. The Higgs field does, however, differ from all other quantum fields in three crucial ways.

The first difference is somewhat technical. All fields have a property called spin, an intrinsic quantity of angular momentum that is carried by each of their particles. Particles such as electrons have spin $1/2$ and most particles associated with a force, such as the photon, have spin 1. The Higgs boson (the particle of the Higgs field) has spin 0. Having 0 spin enables the Higgs field to appear in the Lagrangian in different ways than the other particles do, which in turn allows— and leads to—its other two distinguishing features.

The second unique property of the Higgs field explains how and why it has nonzero strength through-out the universe. Any system, including a universe, will tumble into its lowest energy state, like a ball bouncing down to the bottom of a valley. For the familiar fields, such as the electromagnetic fields that give us radio broadcasts, the lowest energy state is the one in which the fields have zero value (that is, the fields vanish)—if any nonzero field is introduced, the energy stored in the fields increases the net energy of the system. But for the Higgs field, the energy of the universe is lower if the field is not zero but instead has a constant nonzero value. In terms of the valley metaphor, for ordinary

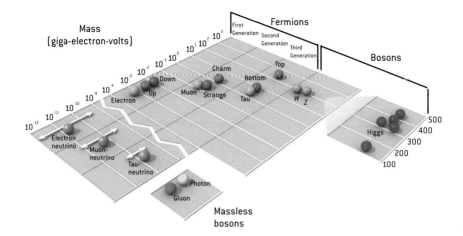

Masses of the particles of the Standard Model differ by at least 11 orders of magnitude and are believed to be generated by interactions with the Higgs field. At least five Higgs particles are likely to exist. Their masses are not known; possible Higgs masses are indicated.

fields the valley floor is at the location of zero field; for the Higgs, the valley has a hillock at its center (at zero field) and the lowest point of the valley forms a circle around the hillock [see "Properties of the Elusive Higgs" box]. The universe, like a ball, comes to rest somewhere on this circular trench, which corresponds to a nonzero value of the field. That is, in its natural, lowest energy state, the universe is permeated throughout by a *nonzero* Higgs field.

The final distinguishing characteristic of the Higgs field is the form of its interactions with the other particles. Particles that interact with the Higgs field behave as if they have mass, proportional to the strength of the field times the strength of the interaction. The masses arise from the terms in the Lagrangian that have the particles interacting with the Higgs field.

Our understanding of all this is not yet complete, however, and we are not sure how many kinds of Higgs fields there are. Although the Standard Model requires only one Higgs field to generate all the elementary particle masses, physicists know that the Standard Model must be superseded by a more complete theory. Leading contenders are extensions of the Standard Model known as Supersymmetric Standard Models (SSMs). In these models, each Standard Model particle has a so-called superpartner (as yet undetected) with closely related properties [see "The Dawn of Physics beyond the Standard Model," by Gordon Kane; *Scientific American*, June 2003]. With the Supersymmetric Standard Model, at least two different kinds of Higgs fields are needed. Interactions with those two fields give mass to the Standard Model particles. They also give some (but not all) mass to the superpartners. The two Higgs fields give rise to five species of Higgs boson: three that are electrically neutral and two that are charged. The masses of particles called neutrinos, which are tiny compared with other particle masses, could arise rather indirectly from these interactions or from yet a third kind of Higgs field.

Theorists have several reasons for expecting the SSM picture of the Higgs interaction to be correct.

First, without the Higgs mechanism, the $W$ and $Z$ bosons that mediate the weak force would be massless, just like the photon (which they are related to), and the weak interaction would be as strong as the electromagnetic one. Theory holds that the Higgs mechanism confers mass to the $W$ and $Z$ in a very special manner. Predictions of that approach (such as the ratio of the $W$ and $Z$ masses) have been confirmed experimentally.

Second, essentially all other aspects of the Standard Model have been well tested, and with such a detailed, interlocking theory it is difficult to change one part (such as the Higgs) without affecting the rest. For example, the analysis of precision measurements of $W$ and $Z$ boson properties led to the accurate prediction of the top quark mass before the top quark had been directly produced. Changing the Higgs mechanism would spoil that and other successful predictions.

Third, the Standard Model Higgs mechanism works very well for giving mass to *all* the Standard Model particles, $W$ and $Z$ bosons, as well as quarks and leptons; the alternative proposals usually do not. Next, unlike the other theories, the SSM provides a framework to unify our understanding of the forces of nature. Finally, the SSM can explain why the energy "valley" for the universe has the shape needed by the Higgs mechanism. In the basic Standard Model the shape of the valley has to be put in as a postulate, but in the SSM that shape can be derived mathematically.

## A Cosmic Stocktaking

The theory of the Higgs field explains how elementary particles, the smallest building blocks of the universe, acquire their mass. But the Higgs mechanism is not the only source of mass-energy in the universe ("mass-energy" refers to both mass and energy, which are related by Einstein's $E = mc^2$).

About 70 percent of the mass-energy of the universe is in the form of so-called dark energy, which is not directly associated with particles. The chief sign of the existence of dark energy is that the universe's expansion is accelerating. The precise nature of dark energy is one of the most profound open questions in physics [see "A Cosmic Conundrum," by Lawrence M. Krauss and Michael S. Turner; *Scientific American*, September 2004].

The remaining 30 percent of the universe's mass-energy comes from matter, particles with mass. The most familiar kinds of matter are protons, neutrons and electrons, which make up stars, planets, people and all that we see. These particles provide about one sixth of the matter of the universe, or 4 to 5 percent of the entire universe. As is explained in the main text, most of this mass arises from the energy of motion of quarks and gluons whirling around inside protons and neutrons.

A smaller contribution to the universe's matter comes from particles called neutrinos, which come in three varieties. Neutrinos have mass but surprisingly little.

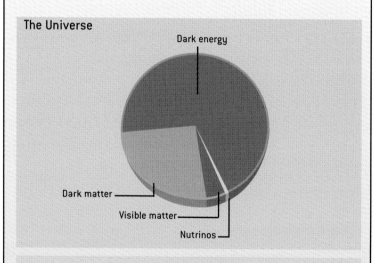

**The Universe**

Dark energy

Dark matter

Visible matter

Nutrinos

The mass-energy of the universe mainly comes in four broad types: mysterious dark energy that causes the universe's expansion to accelerate; invisible dark matter that we can detect by its gravitational effects; visible matter; and neutrinos.

The absolute masses of neutrinos are not yet measured, but the existing data put an upper limit on them—less than half a percent of the universe.

Almost all the rest of the matter—around 25 percent of the universe's total mass-energy—is matter we do not see, called dark matter. We deduce its existence from its gravitational effects on what we do see. We do not yet know what this dark matter actually is, but there are good candidates, and experiments are under way to test different ideas [see "The Search for Dark Matter," by David B. Cline; *Scientific American*, March 2003]. The dark matter should be composed of massive particles because it forms galaxy-sized clumps under the effects of the gravitational force. A variety of arguments have let us conclude that the dark matter cannot be composed of any of the normal Standard Model particles.

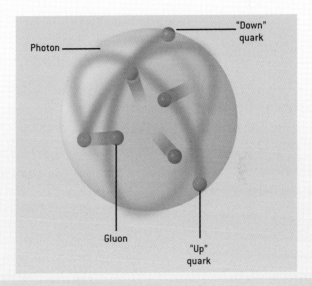

Most visible mass is locked up in protons and neutrons. Each of these consists of quarks and gluons flying around. Almost all of the proton's or neutron's mass is from the energy of motion of the quarks and gluons.

The leading candidate particle for dark matter is the lightest superpartner (LSP), which is discussed in greater detail in the main text. The lightest superpartner occurs in extensions of the Standard Model called Supersymmetric Standard Models. The mass of the LSP is thought to be about 100 proton masses. That the LSP was a good candidate for the dark matter was recognized by theorists before cosmologists knew that a new form of fundamental matter was needed to explain dark matter.

—G. K.

## Testing the Theory

Naturally, physicists want to carry out direct tests of the idea that mass arises from the interactions with the different Higgs fields. We can test three key features. First, we can look for the signature particles called Higgs bosons. These quanta must exist, or else the explanation is not right. Physicists are currently looking for Higgs bosons at the Tevatron Collider at Fermi National Accelerator Laboratory in Batavia, Ill.

Second, once they are detected we can observe how Higgs bosons interact with other particles. The very same terms in the Lagrangian that determine the masses of the particles also fix the properties of such interactions. So we can conduct experiments to test quantitatively the presence of interaction terms of that type. The strength of the interaction and the amount of particle mass are uniquely connected.

Third, different sets of Higgs fields, as occur in the Standard Model or in the various SSMs, imply different sets of Higgs bosons with various properties, so tests can distinguish these alternatives, too. All that we need to carry out the tests are appropriate particle colliders—ones that have sufficient energy to produce the different Higgs bosons, sufficient intensity to make enough of them and very good detectors to analyze what is produced.

A practical problem with performing such tests is that we do not yet understand the theories well enough to calculate what masses the Higgs bosons themselves should have, which makes searching for them more difficult because one must examine a range of masses. A combination of theoretical reasoning and data from experiments guides us about roughly what masses to expect.

The Large Electron-Positron Collider (LEP) at CERN, the European laboratory for particle physics near Geneva, operated over a mass range that had a significant chance of including a Higgs boson. It did not find one—although there was tantalizing evidence for one just at the limits of the collider's energy and intensity—before it was shut down in 2000 to make room for constructing a newer facility, CERN's Large Hadron Collider (LHC). The Higgs must therefore be heavier than about 120 proton masses. Nevertheless, LEP did produce indirect evidence that a Higgs boson exists: experimenters at LEP made a number of precise measurements, which can be combined with similar measurements from the Tevatron and the collider at the Stanford Linear Accelerator Center. The entire set of data agrees well with theory only if certain interactions of particles with the lightest Higgs boson are included and only if the lightest Higgs boson is not heavier than about 200 proton masses. That provides researchers with an upper limit for the mass of the Higgs boson, which helps focus the search.

For the next few years, the only collider that could produce direct evidence for Higgs bosons will be the Tevatron. Its energy is sufficient to discover a Higgs boson in the range of masses implied by the indirect LEP evidence, *if* it can consistently achieve the beam intensity it was expected to have, which so far has not been possible. In 2007 the LHC, which is seven times more energetic and is designed to have far more intensity than the Tevatron, is scheduled to begin taking data. It will be a factory for Higgs bosons (meaning it will produce many of the particles a day). Assuming the LHC functions as planned, gathering the relevant data and learning how to interpret it should take one to two years. Carrying out the complete tests that show in detail that the interactions with Higgs fields are providing the mass will require a new electron-positron collider in addition to the LHC (which collides protons) and the Tevatron (which collides protons and antiprotons).

## Dark Matter

What is discovered about Higgs bosons will not only test whether the Higgs mechanism is indeed providing mass, it will also point the way to how the Standard Model can be extended to solve problems such as the origin of dark matter.

With regard to dark matter, a key particle of the SSM is the lightest superpartner (LSP). Among the superpartners of the known Standard Model particles predicted by the SSM, the LSP is the one with the lowest mass. Most superpartners decay promptly to lower-mass superpartners, a chain of decays that ends with the LSP, which is stable because it has no lighter particle that it can decay into. (When a superpartner decays, at least one of the decay products should be another superpartner; it should not decay entirely into Standard Model particles.) Superpartner particles would have been created early in the big bang but then promptly decayed into LSPs. The LSP is the leading candidate particle for dark matter.

The Higgs bosons may also directly affect the amount of dark matter in the universe. We know that the amount of LSPs today should be less than the amount shortly after the big bang, because some would have collided and annihilated into quarks and leptons and photons, and the annihilation rate may be dominated by LSPs interacting with Higgs bosons.

As mentioned earlier, the two basic SSM Higgs fields give mass to the Standard Model particles and *some* mass to the superpartners, such as the LSP. The superpartners acquire more mass via additional interactions, which may be with still further Higgs fields or with fields similar to the Higgs. We have theoretical models of how these processes can happen, but until we have data on the superpartners themselves we will not know how they work in detail. Such data are expected from the LHC or perhaps even from the Tevatron.

Neutrino masses may also arise from interactions with additional Higgs or Higgs-like fields, in a very interesting way. Neutrinos were originally assumed to be massless, but since 1979 theorists have predicted that they have small masses, and over the past decade several impressive experiments have confirmed the predictions [see "Solving the Solar Neutrino Problem," by Arthur B. McDonald, Joshua R. Klein and David L. Wark; *Scientific American*, April 2003]. The neutrino masses are less than a millionth the size of the next smallest mass, the electron mass. Because neutrinos are electrically neutral, the theoretical description of their masses is more subtle than for charged particles. Several processes contribute to the mass of each neutrino species, and for technical reasons the actual mass value emerges from solving an equation rather than just adding the terms.

Thus, we have understood the three ways that mass arises: The main form of mass we are familiar with—that of protons and neutrons and therefore of atoms—comes from the motion of quarks bound into protons and neutrons. The proton mass would be about what it is even without the Higgs field. The masses of the quarks themselves, however, and also the mass of the electron, are entirely caused by the Higgs field. Those masses would vanish without the Higgs. Last, but certainly not least, most of the amount of superpartner masses, and therefore the mass of the dark matter particle (if it is indeed the lightest superpartner), comes from additional interactions beyond the basic Higgs one.

Finally, we consider an issue known as the family problem. Over the past half a century physicists have shown that the world we see, from people to flowers to stars, is constructed from just six particles: three matter particles (up quarks, down quarks and electrons), two force quanta (photons and gluons), and Higgs bosons— a remarkable and surprisingly simple description. Yet there are four more quarks, two more particles similar to the electron, and three neutrinos. All are very short-lived or barely interact with the other six particles. They can be classified into three families: up, down, electron neutrino, electron; charm, strange, muon neutrino, muon; and top, bottom, tau neutrino, tau. The particles in each family have interactions identical to those of the particles in other families. They differ only in that those in the second family are heavier than those in the first, and those in the third family are heavier still. Because these masses arise from interactions with the Higgs field, the particles must have different interactions with the Higgs field.

Hence, the family problem has two parts: Why are there three families when it seems only one is needed to describe the world we see? Why do the families differ in mass and have the masses they do? Perhaps it is not obvious why physicists are astonished that nature contains three almost identical families even if one would do. It is because we want to fully understand the laws of nature and the basic particles and forces. We expect that every aspect of the basic laws is a necessary one. The goal is to have a theory in which all the particles and their mass ratios emerge inevitably, without making ad hoc assumptions about the values of the masses and without adjusting parameters. If having three families is essential, then it is a clue whose significance is currently not understood.

## Tying It All Together

The Standard Model and the SSM can accommodate the observed family structure, but they cannot explain it. This is a strong statement. It is not that the SSM has not *yet* explained the family structure but that it *cannot*. For me, the most exciting aspect of string theory is not only that it may provide us with a quantum theory of all the forces but also that it may tell us what the elementary particles are and why there are three families. String theory seems able to address the question of why the interactions with the Higgs field differ among the families. In string theory, repeated families can occur, and they are not identical. Their differences are described by properties that do not affect the strong, weak, electromagnetic or gravitational forces but that do affect the interactions with Higgs fields, which fits with our having three families with different masses. Although string theorists have not yet fully solved the problem of having three families, the theory seems to have the right structure to provide a solution. String theory allows many different family structures, and so far no one knows why nature picks the one we observe rather than some other [see "The String Theory Landscape," by Raphael Bousso and Joseph Polchinski; *Scientific American*, September 2004]. Data on the quark and lepton masses and on their superpartner masses may provide major clues to teach us about string theory.

One can now understand why it took so long historically to begin to understand mass. Without the Standard Model of particle physics and the development of quantum field theory to describe particles and their interactions, physicists could not even formulate the right questions. Whereas the origins and values of mass are not yet fully understood, it is likely that the framework needed to understand them is in place. Mass could not have been comprehended before theories such as the Standard Model and its supersymmetric extension and string theory existed. Whether they indeed provide the complete answer is not yet clear, but mass is now a routine research topic in particle physics.

## More to Explore

The Particle Garden. Gordon Kane. Perseus Publishing, 1996.

The Little Book of the Big Bang: A Cosmic Primer. Craig J. Hogan. Copernicus Books, 1998.

Mass without Mass II: The Medium Is the Mass-age. Frank Wilczek in *Physics Today*, Vol. 53, No. 1, pages 13–14; January 2000.

Supersymmetry: Unveiling the Ultimate Laws of Nature. Gordon Kane. Perseus Publishing, 2001.

An excellent collection of particle physics Web sites is listed at **http://particleadventure.org/other/othersites.html**.

## About the Author

*GORDON KANE*, a particle theorist, is Victor Weisskopf Collegiate Professor of Physics at the University of Michigan at Ann Arbor. His work explores ways to test and extend the Standard Model of particle physics. In particular, he studies Higgs physics and the Standard Model's supersymmetric extension and cosmology, with a focus on relating theory and experiment. Recently he has emphasized integrating these topics with string theory and studying the implications for collider experiments.

# 5. "Inconstant Constants"

By John D. Barrow and John K. Webb

*Do the inner workings of nature change with time?*

Some things never change. Physicists call them the constants of nature. Such quantities as the velocity of light, $c$, Newton's constant of gravitation, G, and the mass of the electron, $m_e$, are assumed to be the same at all places and times in the universe. They form the scaffolding around which the theories of physics are erected, and they define the fabric of our universe. Physics has progressed by making ever more accurate measurements of their values.

And yet, remarkably, no one has ever successfully predicted or explained any of the constants. Physicists have no idea why they take the special numerical values that they do. In SI units, $c$ is 299,792,458; G is 6.673 x $10^{-11}$; and $m_e$ is 9.10938188 x $10^{-31}$—numbers that follow no discernible pattern. The only thread running through the values is that if many of them were even slightly different, complex atomic structures such as living beings would not be possible. The desire to explain the constants has been one of the driving forces behind efforts to develop a complete unified description of nature, or "theory of everything." Physicists have hoped that such a theory would show that each of the constants of nature could have only one logically possible value. It would reveal an underlying order to the seeming arbitrariness of nature.

In recent years, however, the status of the constants has grown more muddled, not less. Researchers have found that the best candidate for a theory of everything, the variant of string theory called M-theory, is self-consistent only if the universe has more than four dimensions of space and time—as many as seven more. One implication is that the constants we observe may not, in fact, be the truly fundamental ones. Those live in the full higher-dimensional space, and we see only their three-dimensional "shadows."

Meanwhile physicists have also come to appreciate that the values of many of the constants may be the result of mere happenstance, acquired during random events and elementary particle processes early in the history of the universe. In fact, string theory allows for a vast number—$10^{500}$—of possible "worlds" with different self-consistent sets of laws and constants [see "The String Theory Landscape," by Raphael Bousso and Joseph Polchinski; *Scientific American*, September 2004]. So far researchers have no idea why our combination was selected. Continued study may reduce the number of logically possible worlds to one, but we have to remain open to the unnerving possibility that our known universe is but one of many—a part of a multiverse—and that different parts of the multiverse exhibit different solutions to the theory, our observed laws of nature being merely one edition of many systems of local bylaws [see "Parallel Universes," by Max Tegmark; *Scientific American*, May 2003].

No further explanation would then be possible for many of our numerical constants other than that they constitute a rare combination that permits consciousness to evolve. Our observable universe could be one of many isolated oases surrounded by an infinity of lifeless space— a surreal place where different forces of nature hold sway and particles such as electrons or structures such as carbon atoms and DNA molecules could be impossibilities. If you tried to venture into that outside world, you would cease to be.

Thus, string theory gives with the right hand and takes with the left. It was devised in part to explain the seemingly arbitrary values of the physical constants, and the basic equations of the theory contain few arbitrary parameters. Yet so far string theory offers no explanation for the observed values of the constants.

## A Ruler You Can Trust

Indeed, the word "constant" may be a misnomer. Our constants could vary both in time and in space. If the extra dimensions of space were to change in size, the "constants" in our three-dimensional world would change with them. And if we looked far enough out in space, we might begin to see regions where the

## Overview/Constants of Physics

- The equations of physics are filled with quantities such as the speed of light. Physicists routinely assume that these quantities are constant: they have the same values everywhere in space and time.
- Over the past six years, the authors and their collaborators have called that assumption into question. By comparing quasar observations with laboratory reference measurements, they have argued that chemical elements in the distant past absorbed light differently than the same elements do today. The difference can be explained by a change in one of the constants, known as the fine-structure constant, of a few parts per million.
- Small though it might seem, this change, if confirmed, would be revolutionary. It would mean that the observed constants are not universal and could be a sign that space has extra dimensions.

"constants" have settled into different values. Ever since the 1930s, researchers have speculated that the constants may not be constant. String theory gives this idea a theoretical plausibility and makes it all the more important for observers to search for deviations from constancy.

Such experiments are challenging. The first problem is that the laboratory apparatus itself may be sensitive to changes in the constants. The size of all atoms could be increasing, but if the ruler you are using to measure them is getting longer, too, you would never be able to tell. Experimenters routinely assume that their reference standards—rulers, masses, clocks—are fixed, but they cannot do so when testing the constants. They must focus their attention on constants that have no units— they are pure numbers—so that their values are the same irrespective of the units system. An example is the ratio of two masses, such as the proton mass to the electron mass.

One ratio of particular interest combines the velocity of light, $c$, the electric charge on a single electron, $e$, Planck's constant, $h$, and the so-called vacuum permittivity, $\epsilon_0$. This famous quantity, $\alpha = e^2/2\epsilon_0 hc$, called the fine-structure constant, was first introduced in 1916 by Arnold Sommerfeld, a pioneer in applying the theory of quantum mechanics to electromagnetism. It quantifies the relativistic ($c$) and quantum ($h$) qualities of electromagnetic ($e$) interactions involving charged particles in empty space ($\epsilon_0$). Measured to be equal to 1/137.03599976, or approximately 1/137, $\alpha$ has endowed the number 137 with a legendary status among physicists (it usually opens the combination locks on their briefcases).

If $\alpha$ had a different value, all sorts of vital features of the world around us would change. If the value were lower, the density of solid atomic matter would fall (in proportion to $\alpha^3$), molecular bonds would break at lower temperatures ($\alpha^2$), and the number of stable elements in the periodic table could increase ($1/\alpha$). If $\alpha$ were too big, small atomic nuclei could not exist, because the electrical repulsion of their protons would overwhelm the strong nuclear force binding them together. A value as big as 0.1 would blow apart carbon.

The nuclear reactions in stars are especially sensitive to $\alpha$. For fusion to occur, a star's gravity must produce temperatures high enough to force nuclei together despite

## Light and the Fine-Structure Constant

Several of the best-known constants of nature, including the speed of light, can be combined into the fine-structure constant ($\alpha$)—a number that represents how strongly particles interact through electromagnetic forces. One such interaction is the absorption of photons by atoms. Illuminated by light, an atom absorbs specific colors, each corresponding to photons of a certain wavelength.

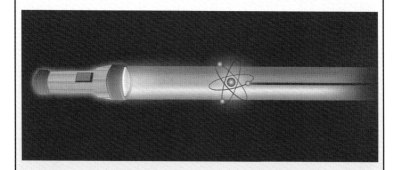

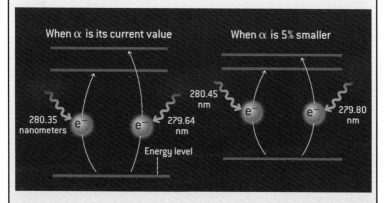

When $\alpha$ is its current value

When $\alpha$ is 5% smaller

280.45 nm

280.35 nanometers

279.64 nm

Energy level

279.80 nm

Energy levels of electrons within the atom describe the absorption process. The energy of a photon is transferred to an electron, which jumps up the ladder of allowable levels. Each possible jump corresponds to a distinct wavelength. The spacing of levels depends on how strongly the electron is attracted to the atomic nucleus and therefore on $\alpha$. In the case of magnesium ions ($Mg^+$), if $\alpha$ were smaller, the levels would be closer together. Photons would need less energy (meaning a longer wavelength) to kick electrons up the ladder.

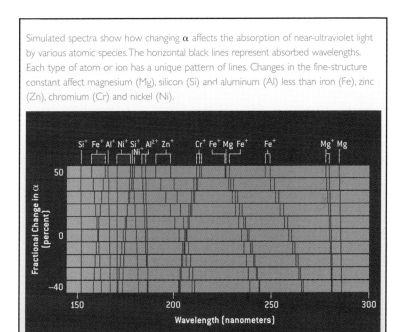

Simulated spectra show how changing α affects the absorption of near-ultraviolet light by various atomic species. The horizontal black lines represent absorbed wavelengths. Each type of atom or ion has a unique pattern of lines. Changes in the fine-structure constant affect magnesium (Mg), silicon (Si) and aluminum (Al) less than iron (Fe), zinc (Zn), chromium (Cr) and nickel (Ni).

their tendency to repel one another. If α exceeded 0.1, fusion would be impossible (unless other parameters, such as the electron-to-proton mass ratio, were adjusted to compensate). A shift of just 4 percent in α would alter the energy levels in the nucleus of carbon to such an extent that the production of this element by stars would shut down.

## Nuclear Proliferation

The second experimental problem, less easily solved, is that measuring changes in the constants requires high-precision equipment that remains stable long enough to register any changes. Even atomic clocks can detect drifts in the fine-structure constant only over days or, at most, years. If $\alpha$ changed by more than four parts in $10^{15}$ over a three-year period, the best clocks would see it. None have. That may sound like an impressive confirmation of constancy, but three years is a cosmic eyeblink. Slow but substantial changes during the long history of the universe would have gone unnoticed.

Fortunately, physicists have found other tests. During the 1970s, scientists from the French atomic energy commission noticed something peculiar about the isotopic composition of ore from a uranium mine at Oklo in Gabon, West Africa: it looked like the waste products of a nuclear reactor. About two billion years ago, Oklo must have been the site of a natural reactor [see "A Natural Fission Reactor," by George A. Cowan; *Scientific American*, July 1976].

In 1976 Alexander Shlyakhter of the Nuclear Physics Institute in St. Petersburg, Russia, noticed that the ability of a natural reactor to function depends crucially on the precise energy of a particular state of the samarium nucleus that facilitates the capture of neutrons. And that energy depends sensitively on the value of $\alpha$. So if the fine-structure constant had been slightly different, no chain reaction could have occurred. But one did occur, which implies that the constant has not changed by more than one part in $10^8$ over the past two billion years.

(Physicists continue to debate the exact quantitative results because of the inevitable uncertainties about the conditions inside the natural reactor.)

In 1962 P. James E. Peebles and Robert Dicke of Princeton University first applied similar principles to meteorites: the abundance ratios arising from the radioactive decay of different isotopes in these ancient rocks depend on $\alpha$. The most sensitive constraint involves the beta decay of rhenium into osmium. According to recent work by Keith Olive of the University of Minnesota, Maxim Pospelov of the University of Victoria in British Columbia and their colleagues, at the time the rocks formed, $\alpha$ was within two parts in $10^6$ of its current value. This result is less precise than the Oklo data but goes back further in time, to the origin of the solar system 4.6 billion years ago.

To probe possible changes over even longer time spans, researchers must look to the heavens. Light takes billions of years to reach our telescopes from distant astronomical sources. It carries a snapshot of the laws and constants of physics at the time when it started its journey or encountered material en route.

## Line Editing

Astronomy first entered the constants story soon after the discovery of quasars in 1965. The idea was simple. Quasars had just been discovered and identified as bright sources of light located at huge distances from

## Looking for Changes in Quasar Light

A distant gas cloud, backlit by a quasar, gives astronomers an opportunity to probe the process of light absorption—and therefore the value of the fine-structure constant—earlier in cosmic history.

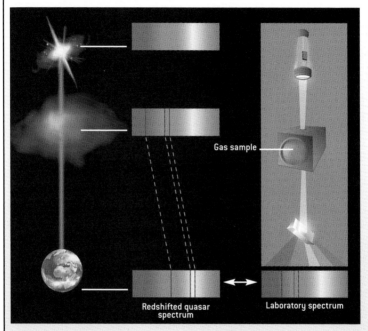

Gas sample

Redshifted quasar
spectrum

Laboratory spectrum

1 Light from a quasar begins its journey to Earth billions of years ago with a smooth spectrum

2 On its way, the light passes through one or more gas clouds. The gas blocks specific wavelengths, creating a series of black lines in the spectrum. For studies of the fine-structure constant, astronomers focus on absorption by metals

3 By the time the light arrives on Earth, the wavelengths of the lines have been shifted by cosmic expansion. The amount of shift indicates the distance of the cloud and, hence, its age

4 The spacing of the spectral lines can be compared with values measured in the laboratory. A discrepancy suggests that the fine-structure constant used to have a different value

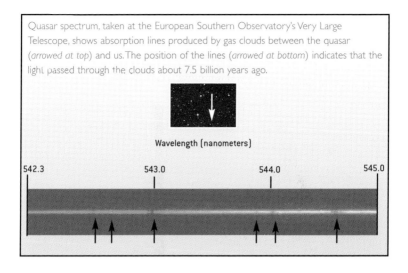

Quasar spectrum, taken at the European Southern Observatory's Very Large Telescope, shows absorption lines produced by gas clouds between the quasar (*arrowed at top*) and us. The position of the lines (*arrowed at bottom*) indicates that the light passed through the clouds about 7.5 billion years ago.

Wavelength (nanometers)

542.3     543.0     544.0     545.0

Earth. Because the path of light from a quasar to us is so long, it inevitably intersects the gaseous outskirts of young galaxies. That gas absorbs the quasar light at particular frequencies, imprinting a bar code of narrow lines onto the quasar spectrum [see "Looking for Changes in Quasar Light" box].

Whenever gas absorbs light, electrons within the atoms jump from a low energy state to a higher one. These energy levels are determined by how tightly the atomic nucleus holds the electrons, which depends on the strength of the electromagnetic force between them— and therefore on the fine-structure constant. If the constant was different at the time when the light was absorbed or in the particular region of the universe where it happened, then the energy required to lift the electron would differ from that required today in laboratory experiments, and the wavelengths of the transitions seen in the spectra would differ. The way in which the wavelengths change depends critically on the orbital configuration of the electrons. For a given change in α, some wavelengths shrink, whereas others increase. The complex pattern of effects is hard to mimic by data calibration errors, which makes the test astonishingly powerful.

Before we began our work seven years ago, attempts to perform the measurement had suffered from two limitations. First, laboratory researchers had not measured the wavelengths of many of the relevant spectral lines with sufficient precision. Ironically, scientists used to know more about the spectra of quasars billions of light-years away than about the spectra of samples here on Earth. We needed high-precision laboratory measurements against which to compare the quasar spectra, so we persuaded experimenters to undertake them. Initial measurements were done by Anne Thorne and Juliet Pickering of Imperial College London, followed by groups led by Sveneric Johansson of Lund Observatory in Sweden and Ulf Griesmann and Rainer Kling of the National Institute of Standards and Technology in Maryland.

The second problem was that previous observers had used so-called alkali-doublet absorption lines—pairs of absorption lines arising from the same gas, such as carbon or silicon. They compared the spacing between these lines in quasar spectra with laboratory measurements. This method, however, failed to take advantage of one particular phenomenon: a change in α shifts not just the spacing of atomic energy levels relative to the lowest-energy level, or ground state, but also the position of the ground state itself. In fact, this second effect is even stronger than the first. Consequently, the highest precision observers achieved was only about one part in $10^4$.

In 1999 one of us (Webb) and Victor V. Flambaum of the University of New South Wales in Australia came up with a method to take both effects into account. The result was a breakthrough: it meant 10 times higher sensitivity. Moreover, the method allows different species (for instance, magnesium and iron) to be compared, which allows additional cross-checks. Putting this idea into practice took complicated numerical calculations to establish exactly how the observed wavelengths depend on α in all different atom types. Combined with modern telescopes and detectors, the new approach, known as the many-multiplet method, has enabled us to test the constancy of α with unprecedented precision.

## Changing Minds

When embarking on this project, we anticipated establishing that the value of the fine-structure constant long ago was the same as it is today; our contribution would simply be higher precision. To our surprise, the first results, in 1999, showed small but statistically significant differences. Further data

## Sometimes It Changes, Sometimes Not

According to the authors' theory, the fine-structure constant should have stayed constant during certain periods of cosmic history and increased during others. The data [see "Measurements" box] are consistent with this prediction.

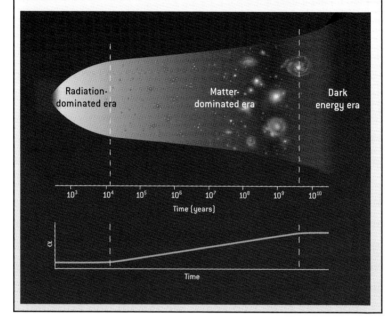

infer the contribution of each. If these abundances in the young universe differed substantially—as might have happened if the stars that spilled magnesium into their galaxies were, on average, heavier than their counterparts today—those differences could simulate a change in $\alpha$.

But a study published this year indicates that the results cannot be so easily explained away. Yeshe

Fenner and Brad K. Gibson of Swinburne University of Technology in Australia and Michael T. Murphy of the University of Cambridge found that matching the isotopic abundances to emulate a variation in α also results in the overproduction of nitrogen in the early universe—in direct conflict with observations. If so, we must confront the likelihood that α really has been changing.

The scientific community quickly realized the immense potential significance of our results. Quasar spectroscopists around the world were hot on the trail and rapidly produced their own measurements. In 2003 teams led by Sergei Levshakov of the Ioffe Physico-Technical Institute in St. Petersburg, Russia, and Ralf Quast of the University of Hamburg in Germany investigated three new quasar systems. Last year Hum Chand and Raghunathan Srianand of the Inter-University Center for Astronomy and Astrophysics in India, Patrick Petitjean of the Institute of Astrophysics and Bastien Aracil of LERMA in Paris analyzed 23 more. None of these groups saw a change in α. Chand argued that any change must be less than one part in 106 over the past six billion to 10 billion years.

How could a fairly similar analysis, just using different data, produce such a radical discrepancy? As yet the answer is unknown. The data from these groups are of excellent quality, but their samples are substantially smaller than ours and do not go as far back in time. The Chand analysis did not fully assess all the experimental and systematic errors—and, being based on a simplified version of the many-multiplet method, might have introduced new ones of its own.

One prominent astrophysicist, John Bahcall of Princeton, has criticized the many-multiplet method itself, but the problems he has identified fall into the category of random uncertainties, which should wash out in a large sample. He and his colleagues, as well as a team led by Jeffrey Newman of Lawrence Berkeley National Laboratory, have looked at emission lines rather than absorption lines. So far this approach is much less precise, but in the future it may yield useful constraints.

## Reforming the Laws

If our findings prove to be right, the consequences are enormous, though only partially explored. Until quite recently, all attempts to evaluate what happens to the universe if the fine-structure constant changes were unsatisfactory. They amounted to nothing more than assuming that $\alpha$ became a variable in the same formulas that had been derived assuming it is a constant. This is a dubious practice. If $\alpha$ varies, then its effects must conserve energy and momentum, and they must influence the gravitational field in the universe. In 1982 Jacob D. Bekenstein of the Hebrew University of Jerusalem was the first to generalize the laws of electromagnetism to handle inconstant constants rigorously. The theory elevates α from a mere number to a so-called scalar field, a dynamic ingredient of nature. His theory did not include gravity, however. Four years ago one of us (Barrow), with Håvard Sandvik and João Magueijo of Imperial College London, extended it to do so. This theory makes appealingly simple predictions. Variations in α of a few parts per million should have a completely negligible effect on the expansion of the universe. That is because electromagnetism is much weaker than gravity on cosmic scales. But although changes in the fine-structure constant do not affect the expansion of the universe significantly, the expansion affects α. Changes to α are driven by imbalances between the electric field energy and magnetic field energy. During the first tens of thousands of years of cosmic history, radiation dominated over charged particles and kept the electric and magnetic fields in balance. As the universe expanded, radiation thinned out, and matter became the dominant constituent of the cosmos. The electric and magnetic energies became unequal, and α started to increase very slowly, growing as the logarithm of time. About six billion years ago dark energy took over and accelerated the expansion, making it difficult for all physical influences to propagate through space. So α became nearly constant again.

This predicted pattern is consistent with our observations. The quasar spectral lines represent the matter-dominated period of cosmic history, when α was increasing. The laboratory and Oklo results fall in the dark-energy-dominated period, during which α has been constant. The continued study of the effect of changing α on radioactive elements in meteorites is particularly interesting, because it probes the transition between these two periods.

## Alpha Is Just the Beginning

Any theory worthy of consideration does not merely reproduce observations; it must make novel predictions. The above theory suggests that varying the fine-structure constant makes objects fall differently. Galileo predicted that bodies in a vacuum fall at the same rate no matter what they are made of—an idea known as the weak equivalence principle, famously demonstrated when Apollo 15 astronaut David Scott dropped a feather and a hammer and saw them hit the lunar dirt at the same time. But if α varies, that principle no longer holds exactly. The variations generate a force on all charged particles. The more protons an atom has in its nucleus, the more strongly it will feel this force. If our quasar observations are correct, then the accelerations of different materials differ by about one part in $10^{14}$—too small to see in the laboratory by a factor of about 100 but large enough to show up in planned missions such as STEP (space-based test of the equivalence principle).

There is a last twist to the story. Previous studies of α neglected to include one vital consideration: the

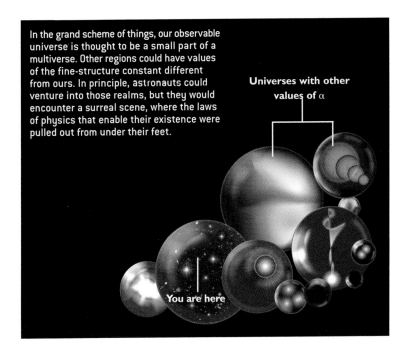

In the grand scheme of things, our observable universe is thought to be a small part of a multiverse. Other regions could have values of the fine-structure constant different from ours. In principle, astronauts could venture into those realms, but they would encounter a surreal scene, where the laws of physics that enable their existence were pulled out from under their feet.

**Universes with other values of $\alpha$**

You are here

lumpiness of the universe. Like all galaxies, our Milky Way is about a million times denser than the cosmic average, so it is not expanding along with the universe. In 2003 Barrow and David F. Mota of Cambridge calculated that $\alpha$ may behave differently within the galaxy than inside emptier regions of space. Once a young galaxy condenses and relaxes into gravitational equilibrium, $\alpha$ nearly stops changing inside it but keeps on changing outside. Thus, the terrestrial experiments that probe the constancy of $\alpha$ suffer from a selection bias. We need to study this effect more to see how it would affect the tests of the weak equivalence principle.

No spatial variations of $\alpha$ have yet been seen. Based on the uniformity of the cosmic microwave background radiation, Barrow recently showed that $\alpha$ does not vary by more than one part in $10^8$ between regions separated by 10 degrees on the sky.

So where does this flurry of activity leave science as far as $\alpha$ is concerned? We await new data and new analyses to confirm or disprove that $\alpha$ varies at the level claimed. Researchers focus on $\alpha$, over the other constants of nature, simply because its effects are more readily seen. If $\alpha$ is susceptible to change, however, other constants should vary as well, making the inner workings of nature more fickle than scientists ever suspected.

The constants are a tantalizing mystery. Every equation of physics is filled with them, and they seem so prosaic that people tend to forget how unaccountable their values are. Their origin is bound up with some of the grandest questions of modern science, from the unification of physics to the expansion of the universe. They may be the superficial shadow of a structure larger and more complex than the three-dimensional universe we witness around us. Determining whether constants are truly constant is only the first step on a path that leads to a deeper and wider appreciation of that ultimate vista.

## More to Explore

**Further Evidence for Cosmological Evolution of the Fine Structure Constant. J. K. Webb, M. T.**

Murphy, V. V. Flambaum, V. A. Dzuba, J. D. Barrow, C. W. Churchill, J. X. Prochaska and A. M. Wolfe in *Physical Review Letters*, Vol. 87, No. 9, Paper No. 091301; August 27, 2001. Preprint available online at **arxiv.org/abs/astro-ph/0012539**.

**A Simple Cosmology with a Varying Fine Structure Constant.** H. B. Sandvik, J. D. Barrow and J. Magueijo in *Physical Review Letters*, Vol. 88, Paper No. 031302; January 2, 2002. **astro-ph/0107512**.

**The Constants of Nature: From Alpha to Omega.** John D. Barrow. Jonathan Cape (London) and Pantheon (New York), 2002.

**Are the Laws of Nature Changing with Time?** J. Webb in *Physics World*, Vol. 16, Part 4, pages 33–38; April 2003.

**Limits on the Time Variation of the Electromagnetic Fine-Structure Constant in the Low Energy Limit from Absorption Lines in the Spectra of Distant Quasars.** R. Srianand, H. Chand, P. Petitjean and B. Aracil in *Physical Review Letters*, Vol. 92, Paper No. 121302; March 26, 2004. **astro-ph/0402177**.

## About the Authors

*JOHN D. BARROW* and *JOHN K. WEBB* began to work together to probe the constants of nature in 1996, when Webb spent a sabbatical with Barrow at the University of Sussex in England. Barrow had been exploring new theoretical possibilities for varying

constants, and Webb was immersed in quasar observations. Their project soon drew in other physicists
and astronomers, notably Victor V. Flambaum of the
University of New South Wales in Australia, Michael
T. Murphy of the University of Cambridge and João
Magueijo of Imperial College London. Barrow is now
a professor at Cambridge and a Fellow of the Royal
Society, and Webb is a professor at New South Wales.
Both are known for their efforts to explain science to
the public. Barrow has written 17 nontechnical books;
his play, *Infinities*, has been staged in Italy; and he has
spoken in venues as diverse as the Venice Film Festival,
10 Downing Street and the Vatican. Webb regularly
lectures internationally and has worked on more than
a dozen TV and radio programs.

# 6. "Quantum Black Holes"

By Bernard J. Carr and Steven B. Giddings

*Physicists could soon be creating black holes in the laboratory.*

Ever since physicists invented particle accelerators, nearly 80 years ago, they have used them for such exotic tasks as splitting atoms, transmuting elements, producing antimatter and creating particles not previously observed in nature. With luck, though, they could soon undertake a challenge that will make those achievements seem almost pedestrian. Accelerators may produce the most profoundly mysterious objects in the universe: black holes.

When one thinks of black holes, one usually envisions massive monsters that can swallow spaceships, or even stars, whole. But the holes that might be produced at the highest-energy accelerators—perhaps as early as 2007, when the Large Hadron Collider (LHC) at CERN near Geneva starts up—are distant cousins of such astrophysical behemoths. They would be microscopic, comparable in size to elementary particles. They would not rip apart stars, reign over galaxies or pose a threat to our planet, but in some respects their properties should be even more dramatic. Because of quantum effects, they would evaporate shortly after they formed, lighting up

## A Tale of Two Black Holes

Astrophysical black holes are thought to be the corpses of massive stars that collapsed under their own weight. As matter falls into them, they act like cosmic hydroelectric plants, releasing gravitational potential energy—the only power source that can account for the intense x-rays and gaseous jets that astronomers see spurting out of celestial systems such as the x-ray binary shown here.

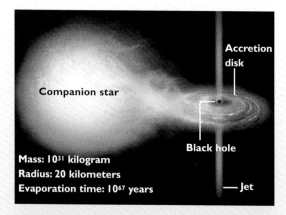

**Accretion disk**

**Companion star**

**Black hole**

**Mass: $10^{31}$ kilogram**
**Radius: 20 kilometers**
**Evaporation time: $10^{67}$ years**

**— Jet**

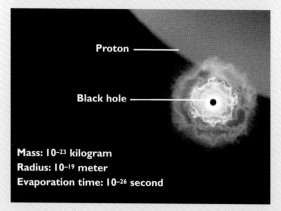

**Proton —**

**Black hole —**

**Mass: $10^{-23}$ kilogram**
**Radius: $10^{-19}$ meter**
**Evaporation time: $10^{-26}$ second**

Microscopic black holes have masses ranging up to that of a large asteroid. They might have been churned out by the collapse of matter early in the big bang. If space has unseen extra dimensions, they might also be created by energetic particle collisions in today's universe. Rather than swallowing matter, they would give off radiation and decay away rapidly.

the particle detectors like Christmas trees. In so doing, they could give clues about how spacetime is woven together and whether it has unseen higher dimensions.

## A Tight Squeeze

In its modern form, the concept of black holes emerges from Einstein's general theory of relativity, which predicts that if matter is sufficiently compressed, its gravity becomes so strong that it carves out a region of space from which nothing can escape. The boundary of the region is the black hole's event horizon: objects can fall in, but none can come out. In the simplest case, where space has no hidden dimensions or those dimensions are smaller than the hole, its size is directly proportional to its mass. If you compressed the sun to a radius of three kilometers, about four-millionths of its present size, it would become a black hole. For Earth to meet the same fate, you would need to squeeze it into a radius of nine millimeters, about a billionth its present size.

Thus, the smaller the hole, the higher the degree of compression that is required to create it. The density to which matter must be squeezed scales as the inverse square of the mass. For a hole with the mass of the sun, the density is about $10^{19}$ kilograms per cubic meter, higher than that of an atomic nucleus. Such a density is about the highest that can be created through gravitational collapse in the present universe. A body lighter than the sun resists collapse because it gets stabilized by

## Overview/Black Hole Factories

- Black holes need not be gargantuan, ravenous monsters. Theory implies that they can come in a huge variety of sizes, some even smaller than subatomic particles. Tiny holes should be wracked by quantum effects, and the very smallest would explode almost as soon as they formed.
- Small black holes might be left over from the early stages of the big bang, and astronomers might be able to detect some of them exploding today.
- Theorists have recently proposed that small black holes might be created in collisions in the present universe, even on Earth. They had thought that the requisite energies were too high, but if space has extra dimensions with the right properties, then the energy threshold for black hole production is much lower. If so, holes might be produced by the Large Hadron Collider (LHC) at CERN and in cosmic-ray collisions high in the atmosphere. Physicists could use the holes to probe the extra dimensions of space.

repulsive quantum forces between subatomic particles. Observationally, the lightest black hole candidates are about six solar masses.

Stellar collapse is not the only way that holes might form, however. In the early 1970s Stephen W. Hawking of the University of Cambridge and one of us (Carr) investigated a mechanism for generating holes in the early universe. These are termed "primordial" black holes. As space expands, the average density of matter decreases; therefore, the density was much higher in the past, in particular exceeding nuclear levels within the first microsecond of the big bang. The known laws of physics allow for a matter density up to the so-called Planck value of $10^{97}$ kilograms per cubic meter—the density at which the strength of gravity becomes so strong that quantum-mechanical fluctuations should break down the fabric of spacetime. Such a density would have been enough to create black holes a mere $10^{-35}$ meter across (a dimension known as the Planck length) with a mass of $10^{-8}$ kilogram (the Planck mass). This is the lightest possible black hole according to conventional descriptions of gravity. It is much more massive but much smaller in size than an elementary particle. Progressively heavier primordial black holes could have formed as the cosmic density fell. Any lighter than $10^{12}$ kilograms would still be smaller than a proton, but beyond this mass the holes would be as large as more familiar physical objects. Those forming during the epoch when the cosmic density matched nuclear density would have a mass comparable to the sun's and so would be macroscopic.

The high densities of the early universe were a prerequisite for the formation of primordial black holes but did not guarantee it. For a region to stop expanding and collapse to a black hole, it must have been denser than average, so density fluctuations were also necessary. Astronomers know that such fluctuations existed, at least on large scales, or else structures such as galaxies and clusters of galaxies would never have coalesced. For primordial black holes to form, these fluctuations must have been stronger on smaller scales than on large ones, which is possible though not inevitable. Even in the absence of fluctuations, holes might have formed spontaneously at various cosmological phase transitions—for example, when the universe ended its early period of accelerated expansion, known as inflation, or at the nuclear density epoch, when particles such as protons condensed out of the soup of their constituent quarks. Indeed, cosmologists can place important constraints on models of the early universe from the fact that not too much matter ended up in primordial black holes.

## Going, Going, Gone?

The realization that holes could be small prompted Hawking to consider what quantum effects might come into play, and in 1974 he came to his famous conclusion that black holes do not just swallow particles but also spit them out [see "The Quantum Mechanics of Black Holes," by S. W. Hawking; *Scientific American*, January 1977]. Hawking predicted that a hole radiates thermally like a hot coal, with a temperature inversely proportional to its mass. For a solar-mass hole, the temperature is around a millionth of a kelvin, which is completely negligible in today's universe. But for a black hole of $10^{12}$ kilograms, which is about the mass of a mountain, it is $10^{12}$ kelvins—hot enough to emit both massless particles, such as photons, and massive ones, such as electrons and positrons.

Because the emission carries off energy, the mass of the hole tends to decrease. So a black hole is highly unstable. As it shrinks, it gets steadily hotter, emitting increasingly energetic particles and shrinking faster and faster. When the hole shrivels to a mass of about $10^6$ kilograms, the game is up: within a second, it

## Ways to Make a Mini Black Hole

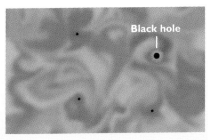

### Primordial density fluctuations

Early in the history of our universe, space was filled with hot, dense plasma. The density varied from place to place, and in locations where the relative density was sufficiently high, the plasma could collapse into a black hole.

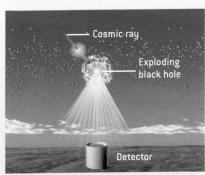

### Cosmic-ray collisions

Cosmic rays—highly energetic particles from celestial sources—could smack into Earth's atmosphere and form black holes. They would explode in a shower of radiation and secondary particles that could be detected on the ground.

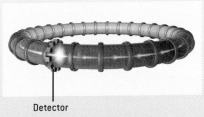

### Particle accelerator

An accelerator such as the LHC could crash two particles together at such an energy that they would collapse into a black hole. Detectors would register the subsequent decay of the hole.

explodes with the energy of a million-megaton nuclear bomb. The total time for a black hole to evaporate away is proportional to the cube of its initial mass. For a solar-mass hole, the lifetime is an unobservably long $10^{64}$ years. For a $10^{12}$-kilogram one, it is $10^{10}$ years—about the present age of the universe. Hence, any primordial black holes of this mass would be completing their evaporation and exploding right now. Any smaller ones would have evaporated at an earlier cosmological epoch.

Hawking's work was a tremendous conceptual advance because it linked three previously disparate areas of physics: general relativity, quantum theory and thermodynamics. It was also a step toward a full quantum theory of gravity. Even if primordial black holes never actually formed, thinking about them has led to remarkable physical insights. So it can be useful to study something even if it does not exist.

In particular, the discovery opened up a profound paradox that aims at the heart of why general relativity and quantum mechanics are so hard to reconcile. According to relativity theory, information about what falls into a black hole is forever lost. If the hole evaporates, however, what happens to the information contained within? Hawking suggested that black holes completely evaporate, destroying the information—in contradiction with the tenets of quantum mechanics. Destruction of information conflicts with the law of energy conservation, making this scenario implausible.

One alternative, that black holes leave behind remnants, is equally unpalatable. For these remnants to encode all the information that could have gone into the black hole, they would have to come in an infinite variety of types. The laws of physics predict that the rate of production of a particle is proportional to the number of types of that particle. Therefore, the black hole remnants would be produced at an infinite rate; even such everyday physical processes as turning on a microwave oven would generate them. Nature would be catastrophically unstable. A third possibility is that locality—the notion that events at spatially separated points can influence one another only after light has had time to travel between them—fails. This conundrum challenges theorists to this day [see "Black Hole Computers," by Seth Lloyd and Y. Jack Ng; *Scientific American*, November 2004].

## Looking for Holes

Progress in physics usually requires some guidance from experiment, so the questions raised by microscopic black holes motivate an empirical search for them. One possibility is that astronomers might be able to detect primordial black holes with an initial mass of $10^{12}$ kilograms exploding in the present universe. Most of the mass of these holes would go into gamma rays. In 1976 Hawking and Don Page, then at the California Institute of Technology, realized that gamma-ray

## The Rise and Demise of a Quantum Black Hole

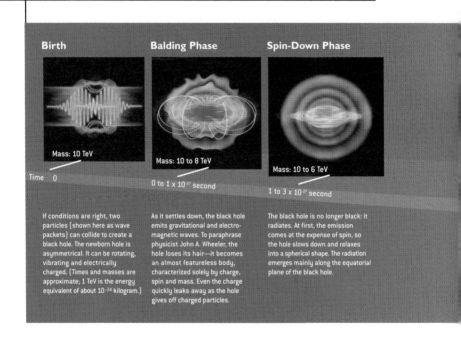

**Birth**

Mass: 10 TeV

Time 0

If conditions are right, two particles (shown here as wave packets) can collide to create a black hole. The newborn hole is asymmetrical. It can be rotating, vibrating and electrically charged. (Times and masses are approximate; 1 TeV is the energy equivalent of about $10^{-24}$ kilogram.)

**Balding Phase**

Mass: 10 to 8 TeV

0 to $1 \times 10^{-27}$ second

As it settles down, the black hole emits gravitational and electro-magnetic waves. To paraphrase physicist John A. Wheeler, the hole loses its hair—it becomes an almost featureless body, characterized solely by charge, spin and mass. Even the charge quickly leaks away as the hole gives off charged particles.

**Spin-Down Phase**

Mass: 10 to 6 TeV

1 to $3 \times 10^{-27}$ second

The black hole is no longer black: it radiates. At first, the emission comes at the expense of spin, so the hole slows down and relaxes into a spherical shape. The radiation emerges mainly along the equatorial plane of the black hole.

background observations place stringent upper limits on the number of such holes. They could not, for example, constitute a significant amount of the universe's dark matter, and their explosions would rarely be close enough to be detectable. In the mid-1990s, however, David Cline of the University of California at Los Angeles and his colleagues suggested that the shortest gamma-ray bursts might be primordial black holes blowing up. Although longer bursts are thought to be associated with exploding or merging stars, the short events may have another explanation. Future observations should settle this issue, but the possibility

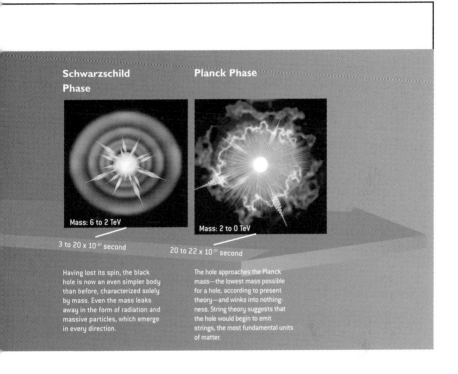

**Schwarzschild Phase**

Mass: 6 to 2 TeV

3 to 20 x 10⁻²⁷ second

Having lost its spin, the black hole is now an even simpler body than before, characterized solely by mass. Even the mass leaks away in the form of radiation and massive particles, which emerge in every direction.

**Planck Phase**

Mass: 2 to 0 TeV

20 to 22 x 10⁻²⁷ second

The hole approaches the Planck mass—the lowest mass possible for a hole, according to present theory—and winks into nothingness. String theory suggests that the hole would begin to emit strings, the most fundamental units of matter.

that astronomical observations could probe the final stages of black hole evaporation is tantalizing.

The production of black holes by particle accelerators is an even more exciting possibility. When it comes to producing high densities, no device outdoes accelerators such as the LHC and the Tevatron at the Fermi National Accelerator Laboratory near Chicago. These machines accelerate subatomic particles, such as protons, to velocities exceedingly close to the speed of light. The particles then have enormous kinetic energies. At the LHC, a proton will reach an energy of roughly seven tera-electron volts (TeV). In accord with Einstein's famous relation $E = mc^2$, this energy is equivalent to a mass of $10^{-23}$ kilogram, or 7,000 times the proton's rest mass. When two such particles collide at close range, their energy is concentrated into a tiny region of space. So one might guess that, once in a while, the colliding particles will get close enough to form a black hole.

As it stands, this argument has a problem: a mass of $10^{-23}$ kilogram is far shy of the Planck value of $10^{-8}$ kilogram, which conventional gravity theory implies is the lightest possible hole. This lower limit arises from the uncertainty principle of quantum mechanics. Because particles also behave like waves, they are smeared out over a distance that decreases with increasing energy— at LHC energies, about $10^{-19}$ meter. So this is the smallest region into which a particle's energy can be packed. It allows for a density of $10^{34}$ kilograms per cubic meter, which is high but not high enough to create a hole. For a particle to be both energetic enough and compact enough to form a black hole, it must have the Planck energy, a factor of $10^{15}$ beyond the energy of the LHC. Although accelerators might create objects mathematically related to black holes (and according to some theorists have already done so), the holes themselves appear to lie out of reach.

## Reaching into Other Dimensions

Over the past decade, however, physicists have realized that the standard estimate of the necessary Planckian density could be too high. String theory, one of the leading contenders for a quantum theory of gravity, predicts that space has dimensions beyond the usual three. Gravity, unlike other forces, should propagate into these dimensions and, as a result, grow unexpectedly stronger at short distances. In three dimensions, the force of gravity quadruples as you halve the distance between two objects. But in nine dimensions, gravity would get 256 times as strong. This effect can be quite important if the extra dimensions of space are sufficiently large, and it has been widely investigated in the past few years [see "The Universe's Unseen Dimensions," by Nima Arkani-Hamed, Savas Dimopoulos and Georgi Dvali; *Scientific American*, August 2000]. There are also other configurations of extra dimensions, known as warped compactifications, that have the same gravity-magnifying effect and may be even more likely to occur if string theory is correct.

This enhanced growth of the strength of gravity means that the true energy scale at which the laws of gravity and quantum mechanics clash—and black holes can be made—could be much lower than its traditional value. Although no experimental evidence yet supports this possibility, the idea sheds light on numerous theoretical conundrums. And if it is true, the density required to create black holes could lie within the range of the LHC.

The theoretical study of black hole production in high-energy collisions goes back to the work of Roger

## Making Holes Is Hard to Do

How much do you need to squeeze a piece of matter to turn it into a black hole? The lighter a body is, the more you must compress it before its gravity becomes strong enough to make a hole. Planets and people are farther from the brink than stars are (*graph*). The wave nature of matter resists compression; particles cannot be squeezed into a region smaller than their characteristic wavelength (*diagram*), suggesting that no hole could be smaller than $10^{-8}$ kilogram. But if space has extra dimensions, gravity would be inherently stronger over short distances and an object would not need to be squeezed as much, giving would-be hole makers hope that they might succeed in the near future.

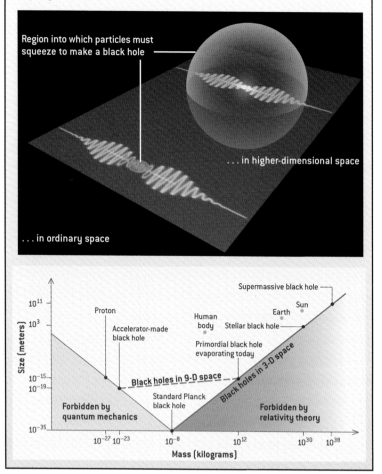

Region into which particles must squeeze to make a black hole

. . . in higher-dimensional space

. . . in ordinary space

Supermassive black hole

Sun

Proton

Human body

Earth

Accelerator-made black hole

Stellar black hole

Primordial black hole evaporating today

Black holes in 9-D space

Black holes in 3-D space

Standard Planck black hole

Forbidden by quantum mechanics

Forbidden by relativity theory

Size (meters)

$10^{11}$

$10^{3}$

$10^{-15}$

$10^{-19}$

$10^{-35}$

$10^{-27}$ $10^{-23}$

$10^{-8}$

$10^{12}$

$10^{30}$ $10^{38}$

Mass (kilograms)

Penrose of the University of Oxford in the mid-1970s and Peter D'Eath and Philip Norbert Payne, both then at Cambridge, in the early 1990s. The newfound possibility of large extra dimensions breathed new life into these investigations and motivated Tom Banks of the University of California at Santa Cruz and Rutgers University and Willy Fischler of the University of Texas to give a preliminary discussion in 1999.

At a 2001 workshop, two groups—one of us (Giddings) with Scott Thomas of Stanford University, and Savas Dimopoulos of Stanford with Greg Landsberg of Brown University—independently described what one would actually see at particle colliders such as the LHC. After a few calculations, we were astounded. Rough estimates indicated that under the most optimistic scenarios, corresponding to the lowest plausible value for the Planck scale, black holes could be produced at the rate of one per second. Physicists refer to an accelerator producing a particle at this rate as a "factory," so the LHC would be a black hole factory.

The evaporation of these holes would leave very distinctive imprints on the detectors. Typical collisions produce moderate numbers of high-energy particles, but a decaying black hole is different. According to Hawking's work, it radiates a large number of particles in all directions with very high energies. The decay products include all the particle species in nature. Several groups have since done increasingly detailed investigations into the remarkable signatures that black holes would produce in the detectors at the LHC.

## Is it Raining Black Holes?

The prospect of producing black holes on Earth may strike some as folly. How do we know that they would safely decay, as Hawking predicted, instead of continuing to grow, eventually consuming the entire planet? At first glance, this seems like a serious concern, especially given that some details of Hawking's original argument may be incorrect—specifically the claim that information is destroyed in black holes. But it turns out that general quantum reasoning implies that microscopic black holes cannot be stable and therefore are safe. Concentrations of mass energy, such as elementary particles, are stable only if a conservation law forbids their decay; examples include the conservation of electric charge and of baryon number (which, unless it is somehow violated, assures the stability of protons). There is no such conservation law to stabilize a small black hole. In quantum theory, anything not expressly forbidden is compulsory, so small black holes will rapidly decay, in accord with the second law of thermodynamics.

Indeed, an empirical argument corroborates that black hole factories would pose no danger. High-energy collisions such as those at the LHC have already taken place—for example, in the early universe and even now, when sufficiently high energy cosmic rays hit our atmosphere. So if collisions at LHC energies can make black holes, nature has already been harmlessly producing them right over our heads. Early estimates

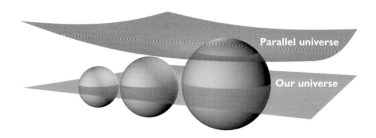

Black holes of different sizes could probe extra dimensions that are otherwise inaccessible to us. Because gravity, unlike other forces, extends into those dimensions, so do black holes. Physicists would vary their size by tuning the particle accelerator to different energies. If a hole intersects a parallel universe, it will decay faster and appear to give off less energy (because some of the energy is absorbed by that other universe).

by Giddings and Thomas indicated that the highest-energy cosmic rays—protons or heavier atomic nuclei with energies of up to $10^9$ TeV—could produce as many as 100 black holes in the atmosphere a year.

In addition, they—along with David Dorfan of U.C. Santa Cruz and Tom Rizzo of the Stanford Linear Accelerator Center and, independently, Jonathan L. Feng of the University of California at Irvine and Alfred D. Shapere of the University of Kentucky—have discovered that collisions of cosmic neutrinos might be even more productive. If so, the new Auger cosmic-ray observatory in Argentina, which is now taking data, and the upgraded Fly's Eye observatory in Utah may be able to see upward of several holes a year. These observations, however, would not obviate the need for accelerator experiments, which could generate holes more reliably, in greater numbers and under more controlled circumstances.

Producing black holes would open up a whole new frontier of physics. Their mere presence would be proof positive of the previously hidden dimensions of space, and by observing their properties, physicists might begin to explore the geographic features of those dimensions. For example, as accelerators manufacture black holes of increasing mass, the holes would poke further into the extra dimensions and could become comparable in size to one or more of them, leading to a distinctive change in the dependence of a hole's temperature on mass. Likewise, if a black hole grows large enough to intersect a parallel three-dimensional universe in the extra dimensions, its decay properties would suddenly change.

Producing black holes in accelerators would also represent the end of one of humankind's historic quests: understanding matter on ever finer scales. Over the past century, physicists have pushed back the frontier of the small—from dust motes to atoms to protons and neutrons to quarks. If they can create black holes, they will have reached the Planck scale, which is believed to be the shortest meaningful length, the limiting distance below which the very notions of space and length probably cease to exist. Any attempt to investigate the possible existence of shorter distances, by performing higher-energy collisions, would inevitably result in black hole production. Higher-energy collisions, rather than splitting matter into finer pieces, would simply produce bigger black holes. In this way, the appearance of black holes would mark the close of a frontier of science. In its place, however, would be a new frontier, that of exploring the geography of the extra dimensions of space.

## More to Explore

**Black Holes and Time Warps: Einstein's Outrageous Legacy.** Kip S. Thorne. W. W. Norton, 1995.

**High Energy Colliders as Black Hole Factories: The End of Short Distance Physics.** Steven B. Giddings and Scott Thomas in *Physical Review D*, Vol. 65, Paper No. 056010; 2002. Preprint available at **arxiv.org/abs/hep-ph/0106219.**

**Black Holes at the LHC.** Savas Dimopoulos and Greg Landsberg in *Physical Review Letters*, Vol. 87, Paper No. 161602; 2001. **hep-ph/0106295.**

**Black Holes from Cosmic Rays: Probes of Extra Dimensions and New Limits on TeV-Scale Gravity.** Luis A. Anchordoqui, Jonathan L. Feng, Haim Goldberg and Alfred D. Shapere in *Physical Review D*, Vol. 65, Paper No. 124027; 2002. **hep-ph/0112247.**

**Black Holes at Accelerators.** Steven B. Giddings in *The Future of Theoretical Physics and Cosmology.* Edited by G. W. Gibbons, E.P.S. Shellard and S. J. Rankin. Cambridge University Press, 2003. **hep-th/0205027.**

**Primordial Black Holes.** Bernard Carr. Ibid. Similar paper available at **astro-ph/0310838**.

## About the Authors

*BERNARD J. CARR* and *STEVEN B. GIDDINGS* first met in person at a conference to celebrate Stephen W. Hawking's 60th birthday in 2002. Carr traces his enthusiasm for astrophysics to the famous 1969 BBC television documentary by Nigel Calder entitled "The Violent Universe." He became a graduate student of Hawking's in the 1970s, was one of the first scientists to investigate small black holes and today is a professor at Queen Mary, University of London. Giddings says he caught the physics bug when his father first told him about the weird properties of quantum mechanics. He went on to become an expert on quantum gravity and cosmology, was among the first to study the possibility of creating black holes in particle accelerators and is now a professor at the University of California, Santa Barbara. When not theorizing about gravity, he defies it by rock climbing.

# "The String Theory
# 7. Landscape"

### By Raphael Bousso and Joseph Polchinski

*The theory of strings predicts that the universe might occupy one random "valley" out of a virtually infinite selection of valleys in a vast landscape of possibilities.*

According to Albert Einstein's theory of general relativity, gravity arises from the geometry of space and time, which combine to form spacetime. Any massive body leaves an imprint on the shape of spacetime, governed by an equation Einstein formulated in 1915. The earth's mass, for example, makes time pass slightly more rapidly for an apple near the top of a tree than for a physicist working in its shade. When the apple falls, it is actually responding to this warping of time. The curvature of spacetime keeps the earth in its orbit around the sun and drives distant galaxies ever farther apart. This surprising and beautiful idea has been confirmed by many precision experiments.

Given the success of replacing the gravitational force with the dynamics of space and time, why not seek a geometric explanation for the other forces of nature and even for the spectrum of elementary particles? Indeed, this quest occupied Einstein for much of his life. He was particularly attracted to work by German Theodor Kaluza and Swede Oskar Klein, which proposed that whereas gravity reflects the shape of the four familiar spacetime dimensions, electromagnetism arises from

Theoretical landscape populated with an array of innumerable possible universes is predicted by string theory. The landscape has perhaps $10^{500}$ valleys, each one of which corresponds to a set of laws of physics that may operate in vast bubbles of space. Our visible universe would be one relatively small region within one such bubble.

the geometry of an additional fifth dimension that is too small to see directly (at least so far). Einstein's search for a unified theory is often remembered as a failure. In fact, it was premature: physicists first had to understand the nuclear forces and the crucial role of quantum field theory in describing physics—an understanding that was only achieved in the 1970s.

The search for a unified theory is a central activity in theoretical physics today, and just as Einstein foresaw, geometric concepts play a key role. The Kaluza-Klein idea has been resurrected and extended as a feature of string theory, a promising framework for the unification of quantum mechanics, general relativity and particle physics. In both the Kaluza-Klein conjecture and string theory, the laws of physics that we see are controlled by the shape and size of additional microscopic dimensions. What determines this shape? Recent experimental and theoretical developments suggest a striking and controversial answer that greatly alters our picture of the universe.

## Kaluza-Klein Theory and Strings

Kaluza and Klein put forth their concept of a fifth dimension in the early part of the 20th century, when scientists knew of two forces—electromagnetism and gravity. Both fall off inversely proportional to the square of the distance from their source, so it was tempting to speculate that they were connected in some way. Kaluza and Klein noticed that Einstein's geometric theory of

## Overview

- According to string theory, the laws of physics that we see operating in the world depend on how extra dimensions of space are curled up into a tiny bundle.
- A map of all possible configurations of the extra dimensions produces a "landscape" wherein each valley corresponds to a stable set of laws.
- The entire visible universe exists within a region of space that is associated with a valley of the landscape that happens to produce laws of physics suitable for the evolution of life.

gravity might provide this connection if an additional spatial dimension existed, making spacetime five-dimensional.

This idea is not as wild as it seems. If the extra spatial dimension is curled up into a small enough circle, it will have eluded our best microscopes—that is, the most powerful particle accelerators [see "Overview" box]. Moreover, we already know from general relativity that space is flexible. The three dimensions that we see are expanding and were once much smaller, so it is not such a stretch to imagine that there is another dimension that remains small today.

Although we cannot detect it directly, a small extra dimension would have important indirect effects that could be observed. General relativity would then describe the geometry of a five-dimensional spacetime. We can split this geometry into three elements: the shape of the four large spacetime dimensions, the angle between the small dimension and the others, and the circumference of the small dimension. The large spacetime behaves according to ordinary four-dimensional general relativity. At every location within it, the angle and circumference have some value, just like two fields permeating spacetime and taking on certain values at each location. Amazingly, the angle field turns out to mimic an electromagnetic field living in the four-dimensional world. That is, the equations governing its behavior are identical to those of electromagnetism. The circumference determines the relative strengths of the electromagnetic and gravitational forces. Thus, from a theory of gravity alone in five dimensions, we obtain a theory of both gravity and electromagnetism in four dimensions.

The possibility of extra dimensions has also come to play a vital role in unifying general relativity and quantum mechanics. In string theory, a leading approach to that unification, particles are in actuality one-dimensional objects, small vibrating loops or strands. The typical size of a string is near the Planck length, or $10^{-33}$ centimeter (less than a billionth of a billionth of the size of an atomic nucleus). Consequently, a string looks like a point under anything less than Planckian magnification.

For the theory's equations to be mathematically consistent, a string has to vibrate in 10 spacetime dimensions, which implies that six extra dimensions exist that are too small to have yet been detected. Along with the strings, sheets known as "branes" (derived from "membranes") of various dimensions can be immersed in spacetime. In the original Kaluza-Klein idea, the quantum wave functions of ordinary particles would fill the extra dimension—in effect, the particles themselves would be smeared across the extra dimension. Strings, in contrast, can be confined to lie on a brane. String theory

## Extra Dimensions/Strings and Tubes

Extra spatial dimensions beyond the three we perceive are postulated by Kaluza-Klein theory and string theory. To imagine those dimensions, which are tiny, consider a space that consists of a long, very thin tube. Viewed from a distance, the tube looks like a one-dimensional line, but under high magnification, its cylindrical shape becomes apparent. Each zero-dimensional point on the line is revealed to be a one-dimensional circle of the tube. In the original Kaluza-Klein theory, every point in our familiar three-dimensional space is actually a tiny circle.

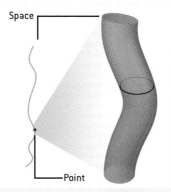

Space

Point

String theory predicts that what appear to be pointlike particles are actually tiny strings. In addition, it predicts the existence of membranelike objects called branes, which can come in a variety of dimensionalities. Strings that have end points always have their ends on a brane. Those that are closed loops are free from that restriction.

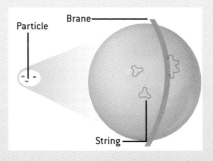

Brane

Particle

String

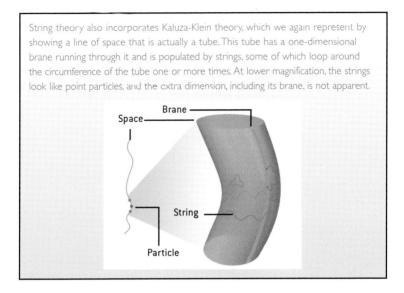

String theory also incorporates Kaluza-Klein theory, which we again represent by showing a line of space that is actually a tube. This tube has a one-dimensional brane running through it and is populated by strings, some of which loop around the circumference of the tube one or more times. At lower magnification, the strings look like point particles, and the extra dimension, including its brane, is not apparent.

also contains fluxes, or forces that can be represented by field lines, much as forces are represented in classical (nonquantum) electromagnetism.

Altogether the string picture looks more complicated than Kaluza-Klein theory, but the underlying mathematical structure is actually more unified and complete. The central theme of Kaluza-Klein theory remains: the physical laws that we see depend on the geometry of hidden extra dimensions.

## Too Many Solutions?

The key question is, What determines this geometry? The answer from general relativity is that spacetime must satisfy Einstein's equations—in the words of John Wheeler of Princeton University, matter tells spacetime how to curve, and spacetime tells matter how to move.

But the solution to the equations is not unique, so many different geometries are allowed. The case of five-dimensional Kaluza-Klein geometry provides a simple example of this nonuniqueness. The circumference of the small dimension can take any size at all: in the absence of matter, four large flat dimensions, plus a circle of any size, solve Einstein's equations. (Similar multiple solutions also exist when matter is present.)

In string theory we have several extra dimensions, which results in many more adjustable parameters. One extra dimension can be wrapped up only in a circle. When more than one extra dimension exists, the bundle of extra dimensions can have many different shapes (technically, "topologies"), such as a sphere, a doughnut, two doughnuts joined together and so on. Each doughnut loop (a "handle") has a length and a circumference, resulting in a huge assortment of possible geometries for the small dimensions. In addition to the handles, further parameters correspond to the locations of branes and the different amounts of flux wound around each loop [see "Vacuum State" box].

Yet the vast collection of solutions are not all equal: each configuration has a potential energy, contributed by fluxes, branes and the curvature itself of the curled-up dimensions. This energy is called the vacuum energy, because it is the energy of the spacetime when the large four dimensions are completely devoid of matter or fields. The geometry of the small dimensions will try to adjust to minimize this energy, just as a ball placed on a slope will start to roll downhill to a lower position.

To understand what consequences follow from this minimization, focus first on a single parameter: the overall size of the hidden space. We can plot a curve showing how the vacuum energy changes as this parameter varies. An example is shown in the top illustration of the "String Landscape" box (see page 151). At very small sizes, the energy is high, so the curve starts out high at the left. Then, from left to right, it dips down into three valleys, each one lower than the previous one. Finally, at the right, after climbing out of the last valley, the curve trails off down a shallow slope to a constant value. The bottom of the leftmost valley is above zero energy; the middle one is at exactly zero; and the right-hand one is below zero.

How the hidden space behaves depends on the initial conditions—where the "ball" that represents it starts on the curve. If the configuration starts out to the right of the last peak, the ball will roll off to infinity, and the size of the hidden space will increase without bound (it will cease to be hidden). Otherwise it will settle down at the bottom of one of the troughs—the size of the hidden space adjusts to minimize the energy. These three local minima differ by virtue of whether the resulting vacuum energy is positive, negative or zero. In our universe the size of the hidden dimensions is not changing with time: if it were, we would see the constants of nature changing. Thus, we must be sitting at a minimum. In particular, we seem to be sitting at a minimum with a slightly positive vacuum energy.

Because there is more than one parameter, we should actually think of this vacuum energy curve as one slice through a complex, multidimensional mountain range, which Leonard Susskind of Stanford University has described as the landscape of string theory [in "String Landscape" box]. The minima of this multidimensional landscape—the bottoms of depressions where a ball could come to rest—correspond to the stable configurations of spacetime (including branes and fluxes), which are called stable vacua.

A real landscape allows only two independent directions (north-south and east-west), and this is all we can draw. But the landscape of string theory is much more complicated, with hundreds of independent directions. The landscape dimensions should not be confused with the actual spatial dimensions of the world; each axis measures not some position in physical space but some aspect of the geometry, such as the size of a handle or the position of a brane.

The landscape of string theory is far from being fully mapped out. Calculating the energy of a vacuum state is a difficult problem and usually depends on finding suitable approximations. Researchers have made steady progress recently, most notably in 2003, when Shamit Kachru, Renata Kallosh and Andrei Linde, all at Stanford, and Sandip Trivedi of the Tata Institute of Fundamental Research in Mumbai, India, found strong evidence that the landscape does have minima where a universe can get stuck.

We cannot be sure how many stable vacua there are—that is, how many points where a ball could rest. But the number could very well be enormous. Some research suggests that there are solutions with up to about 500 handles, but not many more. We can wrap different numbers of flux lines around each handle, but not too many, because they would make the space unstable, like the right part of the curve in the figure. If we suppose that each handle can have from zero to nine flux lines (10 possible values), then there would be $10^{500}$ possible configurations. Even if each handle could have only zero or one flux unit, there are $2^{500}$, or about $10^{150}$, possibilities.

As well as affecting the vacuum energy, each of the many solutions will conjure up different phenomena in the four-dimensional macroscopic world by defining which kinds of particles and forces are present and what masses and interaction strengths they have. String theory may provide us with a unique set of fundamental laws, but the laws of physics that we see in the macroscopic world will depend on the geometry of the extra dimensions.

Many physicists hope that physics will ultimately explain why the universe has the specific laws that it does. But if that hope is to come true, many profound questions about the string theory landscape must be answered. Which stable vacuum describes the physical world we experience? Why has nature chosen this particular vacuum and not any other? Have all other solutions been demoted to mere mathematical possibilities, never to come true? String theory, if correct, would be the ultimate failure in democracy: richly populated with possible worlds but granting the privilege of reality to only one of its many citizens.

## Vacuum State/The Hidden State

Any given solution to the equations of string theory represents a specific configuration of space and time. In particular, it specifies the arrangement of the small dimensions, along with their associated branes and lines of force known as flux lines. Our world has six extra dimensions, so every point of our familiar three-dimensional space hides an associated tiny six-dimensional space, or manifold—a six-dimensional analogue of the circle in the top illustration in the "Extra Dimensions" box. The physics that is observed in the three large dimensions depends on the size and the structure of the manifold: how many doughnutlike "handles" it has, the length and circumference of each handle, the number and locations of its branes, and the number of flux lines wrapped around each doughnut.

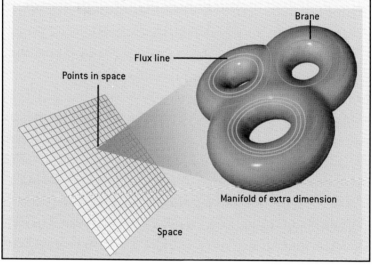

Instead of reducing the landscape to a single chosen vacuum, in 2000 we proposed a very different picture based on two important ideas. The first is that the world need not be stuck with one configuration of the small dimensions for good, because a rare quantum process allows the small dimensions to jump from one configuration to another. The second is that Einstein's general relativity, which is a part of string theory, implies that the universe can grow so rapidly that different configurations will coexist side by side in different subuniverses, each large enough to be unaware of the others. Thus, the mystery of why our particular vacuum should be the only one to exist is eliminated. Moreover, we proposed that our idea resolves one of the greatest puzzles in nature.

## A Trail through the Landscape

As outlined before, each stable vacuum is characterized by its numbers of handles, branes and flux quanta. But now we take into account that each of these elements can be created and destroyed, so that after periods of stability, the world can snap into a different configuration. In the landscape picture, the disappearance of a flux line or other change of topology is a quantum jump over a mountain ridge into a lower valley.

Consequently, as time goes on, different vacua can come into existence. Suppose that each of the 500 handles in our earlier example starts out with nine units of flux. One by one, the 4,500 flux units will decay in some sequence governed by the probabilistic predictions of quantum theory until all the energy stored in fluxes is used up. We start in a high mountain valley and leap randomly over the adjoining ridges, visiting 4,500 successively lower valleys. We are led through some varied scenery, but we pass by only a minuscule fraction of the $10^{500}$ possible solutions. It would seem that most vacua never get their 15 minutes of fame.

Yet we are overlooking a key part of the story: the effect of the vacuum energy on how the universe evolves. Ordinary objects such as stars and galaxies tend to slow down an expanding universe and can even cause it to recollapse. Positive vacuum energy, however, acts like antigravity: according to Einstein's equation, it causes the three dimensions that we see to grow more and more rapidly. This rapid expansion has an important and surprising effect when the hidden dimensions tunnel to a new configuration.

Remember that at every point in our three-dimensional space there sits a small six-dimensional space, which lives at some point on the landscape. When this small space jumps to a new configuration, the jump does not happen at the same instant everywhere. The tunneling first happens at one place in the three-dimensional universe, and then a bubble of the new low-energy configuration expands rapidly [see "String Landscape" box]. If the three large dimensions were not expanding, this growing bubble would eventually overrun every point in the universe. But the old region is also expanding, and this expansion can easily be faster than that of the new bubble.

Everybody wins: both the old and the new regions increase in size. The new never completely obliterates the old. What makes this outcome possible is Einstein's dynamical geometry. General relativity is not a zero-sum game—the stretching of the spatial fabric allows new volume to be created for both the old and the new vacua. This trick will work as the new vacuum ages as well.

When its turn comes to decay, it will not disappear altogether; rather it will sprout a growing bubble, occupied by a vacuum with yet lower energy.

Because the original configuration keeps growing, eventually it will decay again at another location, to another nearby minimum in the landscape. The process will continue infinitely many times, decays happening in all possible ways, with far separated regions losing fluxes from different handles. In this manner, every bubble will be host to many new solutions. Instead of a single sequence of flux decay, the universe thus experiences all possible sequences, resulting in a hierarchy of nested bubbles, or subuniverses. The result is very similar to the eternal inflation scenario proposed by Alan Guth of the Massachusetts Institute of Technology, Alexander Vilenkin of Tufts University, and Linde [see "The Self-Reproducing Inflationary Universe," by Andrei Linde; *Scientific American,* November 1994].

Our scenario is analogous to an infinite number of explorers embarking on all possible paths through every minimum in the landscape. Each explorer represents some location in the universe far away from all the others. The path taken by that explorer is the sequence of vacua experienced at his location in the universe. As long as the explorers' starting point in the landscape is high up in the glaciers, practically all the minima will be visited. In fact, each one will be reached infinitely many times by every possible path downhill from the higher minima. The cascade comes to a halt only where it drops below sea level—into negative energy. The characteristic geometry associated with negative vacuum energy does not allow the game of perpetual expansion and bubble formation to continue. Instead a localized "big crunch" occurs, much like in the interior of a black hole.

In each bubble, an observer conducting experiments at low energies (like we do) will see a specific four-dimensional universe with its own characteristic laws of physics. Information from outside our bubble cannot reach us, because the intermediate space is expanding too rapidly for light to outrun it. We see only one set of laws, those corresponding to our local vacuum, simply because we do not see very far. In our scenario, what we think of as the big bang that began our universe was no more than the most recent jump to a new string configuration in this location, which has now spread across many billions of light-years. One day (probably too far off to worry about) this part of the world may experience another such transition.

## The Vacuum Energy Crisis

The picture we have described explains how all the different stable vacua of the string landscape come into existence at various locations in the universe, thus forming innumerable subuniverses. This result may solve one of the most important and long-standing problems in theoretical physics—one related to the vacuum energy. To Einstein, what we now think of as vacuum energy was an arbitrary mathematical term—a "cosmological constant"—that could be added to his equation of general relativity to make it consistent with his conviction that the universe was static [see "A Cosmic Conundrum," by Lawrence M. Krauss and Michael S. Turner, *Scientific American*, September 2004]. To obtain a static universe, he proposed that this constant takes a positive value, but he abandoned the idea after observations proved the universe to be expanding.

With the advent of quantum field theory, empty space—the vacuum—became a busy place, full of virtual particles and fields popping in and out of existence, and each particle and field carries some positive or negative energy. According to the simplest computations based on this theory, these energies should add up to a tremendous density of about $10^{94}$ grams per cubic centimeter, or one Planck mass per cubic Planck length. We denote that value by $\Lambda p$. This result has been called the most famous wrong prediction in physics because experiments have long shown that the vacuum energy is definitely no greater than $10^{-120}\Lambda p$. Theoretical physics thus stumbled into a major crisis.

Understanding the origin of this great discrepancy has been one of the central goals of theoretical physics for more than three decades, but none of the numerous proposals for a resolution has gained wide acceptance. It was frequently assumed that the vacuum energy is exactly zero—a reasonable guess for a number that is known to have at least 120 zeros after the decimal point. So the apparent task was to explain how physics could produce the value zero. Many attempts centered on the idea that the vacuum energy can adjust itself to zero, but there were no convincing explanations of how this adjustment would take place or why the end result should be anywhere near zero.

In our 2000 paper, we combined the wealth of string theory solutions and their cosmological dynamics with a 1987 insight of Steven Weinberg of the University of Texas at Austin to provide both a how and a why.

First consider the wealth of solutions. The vacuum energy is just the vertical elevation of a point in the landscape. This elevation ranges from around $+\Lambda p$ at the glacial peaks to $-\Lambda p$ at the bottom of the ocean. Supposing that there are $10^{500}$ minima, their elevations will lie randomly between these two values. If we plot all these elevations on the vertical axis, the average spacing between them will be $10^{-500}\Lambda p$. Many, albeit a very small fraction of the total, will therefore have values between zero and $10^{-120}\Lambda p$. This result explains *how* such small values come about.

The general idea is not new. Andrei Sakharov, the late Soviet physicist and dissident, suggested as early as 1984 that the complicated geometries of hidden dimensions might produce a spectrum for vacuum energy that includes values in the experimental window. Other researchers have made alternative proposals that do not seem to be realized in string theory.

We have explained how cosmology populates most of the minima, resulting in a complicated universe that contains bubbles with every imaginable value of the vacuum energy. In which of these bubbles will we find

## String Landscape/Topography of Energy

A landscape emerges when the energy of each possible string solution is plotted as a function of the parameters that define the six-dimensional manifold associated with that solution. If only one parameter is varied—say, the overall size of that manifold—the landscape forms a simple line graph.

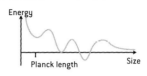

Here three particular sizes (all close to the Planck scale) have energies in the troughs, or minima, of the curve. The manifold will naturally tend to adjust its size to end up at one of the three minima, like a ball rolling around on the slope (it might also "roll off" to infinity at the right-hand end of the graph in this example).

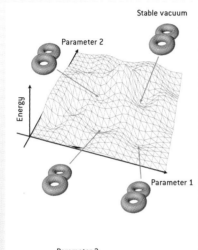

The true string theory landscape reflects all parameters and thus would form a topography with a vast number of dimensions. We represent it by a landscape showing the variation of the energy contained in empty space when only two features change. The manifold of extra dimensions tends to end up at the bottom of a valley, which is a stable string solution, or a stable vacuum— that is, a manifold in a valley tends to stay in that state for a long while.

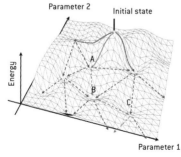

Quantum effects, however, allow a manifold to change state abruptly at some point—to tunnel through the intervening ridge to a nearby lower valley. The red arrows show how one region of the universe might evolve: starting out at a high mountaintop, rolling down into a nearby valley (vacuum A), eventually tunneling through to another, lower valley (vacuum B), and so on. Different regions of the universe will randomly follow different paths. The effect is like an infinite number of explorers traversing the landscape, passing through all possible valleys (dotted arrows).

ourselves? Why should our vacuum energy be so close to zero? Here Weinberg's insight comes into play. Certainly an element of chance is involved. But many places are so inhospitable, it is no wonder we do not live there. This logic is familiar on smaller scale—you were not born in Antarctica, at the bottom of the Marianas Trench or on the airless wastes of the moon. Rather you find yourself in the tiny fraction of the solar system that is hospitable to life. Similarly, only a small fraction of the stable vacua are hospitable to life. Regions of the universe with large positive vacuum energy experience expansions so virulent that a supernova explosion would seem peaceful in comparison. Regions with large negative vacuum energy rapidly disappear in a cosmic crunch. If the vacuum energy in our bubble had been greater than $+10^{-118}\Lambda_p$ or less than $-10^{-120}\Lambda_p$, we could not have lived here, just as we do not find ourselves roasting on Venus or crushed on Jupiter. This type of reasoning is called anthropic.

Plenty of minima will be in the sweet spot, a hair's breadth above or below the water line. We live where we can, so we should not be surprised that the vacuum energy in our bubble is tiny. But neither should we expect it to be exactly zero! About $10^{380}$ vacua lie in the sweet spot, but at most only a tiny fraction of them will be exactly zero. If the vacua are distributed completely randomly, 90 percent of them will be somewhere in the range of 0.1 to $1.0 \times 10^{-118}\Lambda_p$. So if the landscape picture is right, a nonzero vacuum energy should be observed, most likely not much smaller than $10^{-118}\Lambda_p$.

In one of the most stunning developments in the history of experimental physics, recent observations of distant supernovae have shown that the visible universe's expansion is accelerating—the telltale sign of positive vacuum energy [see "Surveying Space-time with Supernovae," by Craig J. Hogan, Robert P. Kirshner and Nicholas B. Suntzeff; *Scientific American,* January 1999]. From the rate of acceleration, the value of the energy was determined to be about $10^{-120}\Lambda p$, just small enough to have evaded detection in other experiments and large enough for the anthropic explanation to be plausible.

The landscape picture seems to resolve the vacuum energy crisis, but with some unsettling consequences. Einstein asked whether God had a choice in how the universe was made or whether its laws are completely fixed by some fundamental principle. As physicists, we might hope for the latter. The underlying laws of string theory, although they are still not completely known, appear to be completely fixed and inevitable: the mathematics does not allow any choices. But the laws that we see most directly are not the underlying laws. Rather our laws depend on the shape of the hidden dimensions, and for this the choices are many. The details of what we see in nature are not inevitable but are a consequence of the particular bubble that we find ourselves in.

Does the string landscape picture make other predictions, beyond the small but nonzero value of the vacuum energy? Answering this question will require a much greater understanding of the spectrum of vacua and is the subject of active research on several fronts. In particular, we have not yet located a specific stable vacuum that reproduces the known laws of physics in our four-dimensional spacetime. The string landscape is largely uncharted territory. Experiments could help. We might someday see the higher-dimensional physical laws directly, via strings, black holes or Kaluza-Klein particles using accelerators. Or we might even make direct astronomical observations of strings of cosmic size, which could have been produced in the big bang and then expanded along with the rest of the universe.

The picture that we have presented is far from certain. We still do not know the precise formulation of string theory—unlike general relativity, where we have a precise equation based on a well-understood underlying physical principle, the exact equations of string theory are unclear, and important physical concepts probably remain to be discovered. These may completely change or do away with the landscape of string vacua or with the cascade of bubbles that populate the landscape. On the experimental side, the existence of nonzero vacuum energy now seems an almost inevitable conclusion from observations, but cosmological data are notoriously fickle and surprises are still possible.

It is far too early to stop seeking competing explanations for the existence of vacuum energy and its very small size. But it would be equally foolish to dismiss the possibility that we have emerged in one of the gentler corners of a universe more varied than all the landscapes of planet Earth.

## More to Explore

**The Elegant Universe. Brian Greene.** W. W. Norton, 1999.

**A First Course in String Theory. Barton Zwiebach.** Cambridge University Press, 2004.

**The Cosmological Constant Problem.** Thomas Banks in *Physics Today*, Vol. 57, No. 3, pages 46–51; March 2004.

The official string theory Web site is at **www.superstringtheory.com.**

## About the Authors

*RAPHAEL BOUSSO* and *JOSEPH POLCHINSKI'S* work together began at a workshop on string duality in Santa Barbara. It grew out of the synergy between Bousso's background in quantum gravity and inflationary cosmology and Polchinski's background in string theory. Bousso is assistant professor of physics at the University of California, Berkeley. His research includes a general formulation of the holographic principle, which relates spacetime geometry to its information content. Polchinski is a professor at the Kavli Institute for Theoretical Physics at the University of California, Santa Barbara. His contributions to string theory include the seminal idea that branes constitute a significant feature of the theory.

# Web Sites

Due to the changing nature of Internet links, Rosen Publishing has developed an online list of Web sites related to the subject of this book. This site is updated regularly. Please use this link to access the list:

http://www.rosenlinks.com/saces/beex

# For Further Reading

Baumann, Mary K., Will Hopkins, Loralee Nolletti, and Michael Soluri. *What's Out There: Images from Here to the Edge of the Universe.* London, England: Duncan Baird, 2005.

"The Elegant Universe." NOVA Science Programming on Air and Online. Retrieved June 20, 2007 (http://www.pbs.org/wgbh/nova/elegant/).

Ford, Kenneth W. *The Quantum World: Quantum Physics for Everyone.* Cambridge, MA: Harvard University Press, 2004.

Fox, Karen C. *The Big Bang Theory: What It Is, Where It Came From, and Why It Works.* New York, NY: Wiley, 2002.

Greene, Brian. *The Elegant Universe: Superstrings, Hidden Dimensions, and the Quest for the Ultimate Theory.* New York, NY: Vintage, 2000.

Greene, Brian. *The Fabric of the Cosmos: Space, Time, and the Texture of Reality.* New York, NY: A. A. Knopf, 2004.

Halpern, Paul. *The Great Beyond: Higher Dimensions, Parallel Universes and the Extraordinary Search for a Theory of Everything.* Hoboken, NJ: Wiley, 2004.

Smolin, Lee. *Three Roads to Quantum Gravity*, reprint ed. New York, NY: Basic Books, 2001.

Smolin, Lee. *The Trouble with Physics: The Rise of String Theory, the Fall of a Science, and What Comes Next.* New York, NY: Houghton Mifflin, 2006.

Thorne, Kip S. *Black Holes and Time Warps: Einstein's Outrageous Legacy.* New York, NY: W. W. Norton & Company, 1995.

Tyson, Neil deGrasse. *Death by Black Hole: And Other Cosmic Quandaries.* New York, NY: W. W. Norton & Company, 2007.

Wheeler, J. Craig. *Cosmic Catastrophes: Exploding Stars, Black Holes, and Mapping the Universe.* Cambridge, England: Cambridge University Press, 2007.

# INDEX